Triple Irish Chain Quilts

by Wendy Gilbert

a Quilt in a Day® Publication

For Grandma…
Who taught me the joy and love of sewing

First printing July, 1997

Published by Quilt in a Day®, Inc.
1955 Diamond St. San Marcos, CA 92069

©1997 by Wendy Gilbert

ISBN 0-922705-93-3

Editor Eleanor Burns
Art Director Merritt Voigtlander
Production Assistant Robin Green

Table of Contents

Introduction

Wendy Gilbert

I t's been over 40 years since my Grandmother, Zelda Cannon, and I spent afternoons sewing. When I was very small, Grandma did most of the sewing while I stood by her side handing her scissors and cutting threads. It wasn't long, however, before I was big enough to work the treadle on Grandma's sewing machine. My favorite projects were Barbie doll clothes fashioned from fabric scraps Grandma had saved from one of her many projects.

My Grandmother instilled in me an enormous love for sewing. This love developed into what I call my unconditional love for quilting. I often compare it to the unconditional love a grandmother has for a grandchild. I love everything about quilting! I love the friendly people that I have met all over the country, always willing to share their quilting expertise. I love the wealth of designs available to help plan my next project. I love the excitement of fabric shopping and the thrill of finding the "perfect" fabric. I love teaching and taking new classes where I learn new techniques and meet new quilters. I love going to quilt shows for inspiration. But most of all, I love to sew quilts.

My inspiration for the first Triple Irish Chain Quilt came from the antique quilt shown here. The quilt began as a tribute to my Grandmother who taught me to sew with scraps and now has grown into this new book with three wonderful patterns. My Grandmother would be delighted that I am passing along my love of quilting to others just as she passed along her love of sewing to me.

Zelda Cannon

Choosing Your Pattern

There are three different Triple Irish Chain patterns to choose from:

Three Color Chain

Yankee Chain

Scrap Chain

All three patterns are created using strips and the same strip sewing techniques. The difference between each pattern is the fabric selection and color placement. Choose the pattern that most appeals to you!

Three Color Chain

The Three Color Chain has the traditional look of a Triple Irish Chain quilt. Three different fabrics make up the chain.

Top Right In this lap quilt, **Color One**, burgundy, is the focus fabric, creating the "X" running through the center of the chain and along the outside of the **Seminole border**. **Color Two**, a floral, makes up the inside two rows of the chain. **Color Three**, blue, makes up the outside two rows of the chain. The three colors of the chain are repeated in the **Seminole Border**. Both the **Framing Border** and the **Outside Border** are made of the light background fabric.

Bottom Right A **Three Color Chain** takes on a completely different look with a pretty blue floral as the **Background**. The springtime green of **Color One** is highlighted by a light fabric for **Color Two** and framed by a pink quilter's suede for **Color Three**.

Eleanor Burns and Cynthia Martin

Sue Bouchard

5

Yankee Chain

The Yankee Chain is a combination of the Three Color Chain and the Scrap Chain.

Top Right In this quilt, reproduction fabrics are used in the center three rows of the chain. One **Dominant Color**, a burgundy, runs the length of the chain along the two outside rows. Medium contrast between the dominant and the scrap fabrics give the quilt a quiet, warm look.

Teresa Varnes

Bottom Right Bright and cheerful scraps contrast with the pink **Dominant Fabric** on either side of the chain, producing the look of a mock Postage Stamp Quilt.

Eleanor Burns and the Methods Update Class

Scrap Chain

The Scrap Chain uses 57 different scrap strips in both the Chain and Seminole border.

Right This vibrant lap size Amish quilt is the result of high contrast between the **Scrap Chain Fabrics** and the black **Background**.

Bottom Right A white **Background** gives a clear fresh look to the quilt. Movement is also created by using directional fabrics.

Bottom Left A more muted quilt is produced by using fabrics similar in value that blend together with the softer tan background.

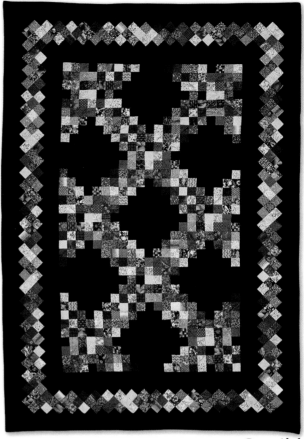

Betty Abel

LouAnn Engelhardt

Ann Nowak

7

Fabric Selection

Fabric

Chain fabrics must be 100% cotton at least 42" wide that are consistently the same weight. If you are using fabrics from your stash, and you are not sure they are all 100% cotton, you may wish to use the burn test. Cotton fabrics burn like paper but fabrics with any polyester melt and leave a hard edge.

Because Irish Chain quilts typically have a lot of contrast between the background fabric and the chain fabrics, it is important to prewash your chain fabric to remove any excess dyes that might bleed into a lighter area when the quilt is laundered. It may be difficult to know whether a scrap fabric has been prewashed. If in doubt, you may choose to sew the quilt and then wash it afterwards. Refer to laundering instructions on page 78 for washing the finished quilt.

Choose your **background fabric** carefully. Directional prints and one-way designs are not suitable. Consider how you will quilt the top when finished. A solid light color or tone on tone fabric will show off your quilting whereas a larger scale print or dark background tends to hide quilting stitches.

Consider **backing fabric** that is similar in color to your background fabric. This will eliminate the problem of backing fabric altering the look of the quilt top. It also helps to hide machine quilting threads better. It's best if you purchase your backing after your quilt top is finished and measured.

Batting

Before purchasing any batting, consider how you want your finished quilt to look. To achieve the look of an old antique quilt, use a cotton or cotton/polyester 80/20 batting. Do not pre-wash the batting. The cotton batting will shrink slightly after the completed quilt is washed, giving it an antique appearance. (See page 78.) Quilting lines need to be a minimum of 3" apart, preferably closer. If you do not plan on shrinking your quilt, then a polyester batting can be used. Polyester batting requires less quilting and will not shrink when washed. A low loft batting is suggested so the quilt will fit through the keyhole of your sewing machine. Wait until after your quilt is finished and measured to purchase your batting.

Customizing Bed Size Quilts

The Yardage and Cutting charts are based on standard mattress sizes. The block portion of the quilt is planned to cover the mattress top with the three borders hanging over the side. Do not alter the block portion of the quilt because the Seminole border is made to fit the number of blocks in a particular size quilt.

The approximate size listed on the Yardage chart is labeled "approximate" because seam sizes differ from quilter to quilter. Machine quilting "shrinks" the size. Washing the quilt for an antique look will also shrink it, anywhere from 2" to 5" in length and width.

Supplies

Rotary Cutter

18" x 24" Cutting Mat

Pressing Mat

Sew Perfect™

Stiletto

6" x 12" Ruler   16" Square Up   6" x 24" Ruler

Quilter's Pins

Seam Guide

1" Safety Pins

Continuous Line Stencil
by Harriet Hargrave

Walking Foot
Darning Foot

Cellophane
Tape

Fine Line Pencil

Binder Clamps

Hera Marker

Kwik Klip™

Jaws™

Orvus & Retayne

Quilt Sew Easy™

Invisible Thread

Thread to blend

Baby Quilt Wallhanging

Approximate Size 61" x 61"
5 A Blocks – 4 B Blocks
Total of Blocks 9
Choose 100% cotton fabric, at least 42" wide.

Eleanor Burns and Wendy Gilbert

Three Color Chain Example

Wendy and Eleanor teamed up to make this lovely three color wall-hanging. The chain design is strong with an energetic pink fabric used as Color One.

Purchase Yardage	Cut Strips, then…	…Separate Into Two Groups	

Three Color Chain

Purchase Yardage	Cut Strips, then…	Blocks	Seminole Border
Color 1 – ¾ yd	(10) 2¼" x 42" strips Cut 5 strips in thirds	(13) 2¼" x 14" strips	(5) 2¼" x 42" strips
Color 2 – 1 yd	(13) 2¼" x 42" strips Cut 8 strips in thirds	(24) 2¼" x 14" strips	(5) 2¼" x 42" strips
Color 3 – 1 yd	(12) 2¼" x 42" strips Cut 7 strips in thirds	(20) 2¼" x 14" strips	(5) 2¼" x 42" strips
Background – 2½ yds	(12) 2¼" x 42" strips Cut 2 strips in thirds	(4) 2¼" x 14" strips	(10) 2¼" x 42" strips
Cut Block B and Outside Border Later	**Framing Border** (4) 2¼" x 42" strips		
Binding – ¾ yd	(6) 3" x 42" strips		
Backing – 3⅔ yds	2 equal pieces		
Batting	66" x 66"		

Yankee Chain

Purchase Yardage	Cut Strips, then…	Blocks	Seminole Border
37 Different Fabrics	(1) 2¼" x 42" strip from each Cut each strip in thirds	(37) 2¼" x 14" strips	(32) 2¼" x 14" strips
Dominant Chain Fabric 1 yd	(12) 2¼" x 42" strips Cut each strip in thirds	(20) 2¼" x 14" strips	(16) 2¼" x 14" strips
Background 2¼ yds	(12) 2¼" x 42" strips Cut each strip in thirds	(4) 2¼" x 14" strips	(32) 2¼" x 14" strips
Cut Block B and Outside Border Later	**Framing Border** (4) 2¼" x 42" strips		
Binding – ¾ yd	(6) 3" x 42" strips		
Backing – 3⅔ yds	2 equal pieces		
Batting	66" x 66"		

Scrap Chain

Purchase Yardage	Cut Strips, then…	Blocks	Seminole Border
57 Different Fabrics	(1) 2¼" x 42" strip from each Cut each strip in thirds	(57) 2¼" x 14" strips	(48) 2¼" x 14" strips
Background 2¼ yds	(12) 2¼" x 42" strips Cut each strip in thirds	(4) 2¼" x 14" strips	(32) 2¼" x 14" strips
Cut Block B and Outside Border Later	**Framing Border** (4) 2¼" x 42" strips		
Binding – ¾ yd	(6) 3" x 42" strips		
Backing – 3⅔ yds	2 equal pieces		
Batting	66" x 66"		

Lap Robe

Approximate Size 61" x 85"
8 A Blocks – 7 B Blocks
Total of Blocks 15
Choose 100% cotton fabric, at least 42" wide.

Lee Codington

Scrap Chain Example

An all-blue color scheme and a white background give this lap robe the delicate look of Dresden china. The Seminole border alternates scrap fabrics with a single dark blue to anchor them.

Purchase Yardage	Cut Strips, then...	...Separate Into Two Groups	
Three Color Chain	Cut strips selvage to selvage	**Blocks**	**Seminole Border**
Color 1 – 1 yd	(14) 2¼" x 42" strips	(13) 2¼" x 21" strips	(14) 2¼" x 21" strips
Color 2 – 1⅓ yds	(19) 2¼" x 42" strips	(24) 2¼" x 21" strips	(14) 2¼" x 21" strips
Color 3 – 1¼ yds	(17) 2¼" x 42" strips	(20) 2¼" x 21" strips	(14) 2¼" x 21" strips
	Cut each strip in half		
Background – 4 yds	(16) 2¼" x 42" strips	(4) 2¼" x 21" strips	(28) 2¼" x 21" strips
	Cut each strip in half		
Cut Block B and Outside Border Later	**Framing Border**		
	(6) 4" x 42" strips		
Binding – ¾ yd	(7) 3" x 42" strips		
Backing – 3¾ yds	2 equal pieces		
Batting	66" x 90"		
Yankee Chain	Cut strips selvage to selvage	**Blocks**	**Seminole Border**
37 Different Fabrics	(1) 2¼" x 42" strip from each	(37) 2¼" x 21" strips	(28) 2¼" x 21" strips
	Cut each strip in half		
Dominant Chain Fabric 1¼ yds	(17) 2¼" x 42" strips	(20) 2¼" x 21" strips	(14) 2¼" x 21" strips
	Cut each strip in half		
Background 4 yds	(16) 2¼" x 42" strips	(4) 2¼" x 21" strips	(28) 2¼" x 21" strips
	Cut each strip in half		
Cut Block B and Outside Border Later	**Framing Border**		
	(6) 4" x 42" strips		
Binding – ¾ yd	(7) 3" x 42" strips		
Backing – 3¾ yds	2 equal pieces		
Batting	66" x 90"		
Scrap Chain	Cut strips selvage to selvage	**Blocks**	**Seminole Border**
57 Different Fabrics	(1) 2¼" x 42" strip from each	(57) 2¼" x 21" strips	(42) 2¼" x 21" strips
	Cut each strip in half		
Background 4 yds	(16) 2¼" x 42" strips	(4) 2¼" x 21" strips	(28) 2¼" x 21" strips
	Cut each strip in half		
Cut Block B and Outside Border Later	**Framing Border**		
	(6) 4" x 42" strips		
Binding – ¾ yd	(7) 3" x 42" strips		
Backing – 3¾ yds	2 equal pieces		
Batting	66" x 90"		

Twin

Approximate Size 68" x 104"
9 A Blocks – 9 B Blocks
Total of Blocks 18
Choose 100% cotton fabric, at least 42" wide.

Emily Dolfin

Yankee Chain Example

Emily made a Yankee Chain with a twist – she chose different fabrics in the same color family for the center chain. She dyed her quilt a light tan, then laundered it to give a mellow look.

Purchase Yardage	Cut Strips, then...	...Separate Into Two Groups	

Three Color Chain

Purchase Yardage	Cut Strips, then...	Blocks	Seminole Border
Three Color Chain	Cut strips selvage to selvage		
Color 1 – 1¼ yds	(16) 2¼" x 42" strips	(13) 2¼" x 24" strips	(16) 2¼" x 18" strips
Color 2 – 1¾ yds	(24) 2¼" x 42" strips	(24) 2¼" x 24" strips	(16) 2¼" x 18" strips
Color 3 – 1½ yds	(20) 2¼" x 42" strips	(20) 2¼" x 24" strips	(16) 2¼" x 18" strips
	Cut each strip at 24"		
Background 5½ yds	(18) 2¼" x 42" strips	(4) 2¼" x 24" strips	(32) 2¼" x 18" strips
	Cut 4 strips at 24"		
	Cut remainder at 18"		
Cut Block B and Outside Border Later	**Framing Border** (7) 4" x 42" strips		
Binding – 1 yd	(9) 3" x 42" strips		
Backing – 6 yds	2 equal pieces		
Batting	72" x 108"		

Yankee Chain

Purchase Yardage	Cut Strips, then...	Blocks	Seminole Border
Yankee Chain	Cut strips selvage to selvage		
37 Different Fabrics	(1) 2¼" x 42" strips from each	(37) 2¼" x 24" strips	(32) 2¼" x 18" strips
	Cut each strip at 24"		
Dominant Chain Fabric 1½ yds	(20) 2¼" x 42" strips	(20) 2¼" x 24" strips	(16) 2¼" x 18" strips
	Cut each strip at 24"		
Background 5½ yds	(18) 2¼" x 42" strips	(4) 2¼" x 24" strips	(32) 2¼" x 18" strips
	Cut 4 strips at 24"		
	Cut remainder at 18"		
Cut Block B and Outside Border Later	**Framing Border** (7) 4" x 42" strips		
Binding – 1 yd	(9) 3" x 42" strips		
Backing – 6 yds	2 equal pieces		
Batting	72" x 108"		

Scrap Chain

Purchase Yardage	Cut Strips, then...	Blocks	Seminole Border
Scrap Chain	Cut strips selvage to selvage		
57 Different Fabrics	(1) 2¼" x 42" strip from each	(57) 2¼" x 24" strips	(48) 2¼" x 18" strips
	Cut each strip at 24"		
Background 5½ yds	(18) 2¼" x 42" strips	(4) 2¼" x 24" strips	(32) 2¼" x 18" strips
	Cut 4 strips at 24"		
	Cut remainder at 18"		
Cut Block B and Outside Border Later	**Framing Border** (7) 4" x 42" strips		
Binding – 1 yd	(9) 3" x 42" strips		
Backing – 6 yds	2 equal pieces		
Batting	72" x 108"		

Double
Queen

Double Approximate Size 88" x 113"
   Outside Border 5½"
Queen Approximate Size 92" x 117"
   Outside Border 7½"
18 A Blocks – 17 B Blocks
Total of Blocks 35
Choose 100% cotton fabric, at least 42" wide.

Vonnie Landwehr

Scrap Chain Example

Intricate machine quilting in the B blocks and borders shows up beautifully on a light fabric. Vonnie used a wide range of colors for a very scrappy look. Yellow and red fabrics add a vibrant touch.

Purchase Yardage	Cut Strips, then…	…Separate Into Two Groups	

Three Color Chain

Purchase Yardage	Cut Strips, then…	Blocks	Seminole Border
Color 1 – 1¾ yds	**Cut strips selvage to selvage** (21) 2¼" x 42" strips	(13) 2¼" x 42" strips	(8) 2¼" x 42" strips
Color 2 – 2¼ yds	(32) 2¼" x 42" strips	(24) 2¼" x 42" strips	(8) 2¼" x 42" strips
Color 3 – 2 yds	(28) 2¼" x 42" strips	(20) 2¼" x 42" strips	(8) 2¼" x 42" strips
Background 6½ yds	(20) 2¼" x 42" strips	(4) 2¼" x 42" strips	(16) 2¼" x 42" strips
Cut Block B and *Outside Border Later*	**Framing Border** (8) 4" x 42" strips		
Binding – 1 yd	(11) 3" x 42" strips		
Backing – 8¼ yds	3 equal pieces		
Batting	Double 94" x 118" Queen 94" x 120"		

Yankee Chain

Purchase Yardage	Cut Strips, then…	Blocks	Seminole Border
37 Different Fabrics	**Cut strips selvage to selvage** (2) 2¼" x 42" strips from each Cut 1 strip of each in half	(37) 2¼" x 42" strips	(36) 2¼" x 21" strips
Dominant Chain Fabric 2 yds	(29) 2¼" x 42" strips Cut 9 strips in half	(20) 2¼" x 42" strips	(18) 2¼" x 21" strips
Background 6½ yds	(22) 2¼" x 42" strips Cut 18 strips in half	(4) 2¼" x 42" strips	(36) 2¼" x 21" strips
Cut Block B and *Outside Border Later*	**Framing Border** (8) 4" x 42" strips		
Binding – 1 yd	(11) 3" x 42" strips		
Backing – 8¼ yds	3 equal pieces		
Batting	Double 94" x 118" Queen 98" x 120"		

Scrap Chain

Purchase Yardage	Cut Strips, then…	Blocks	Seminole Border
57 Different Fabrics	**Cut strips selvage to selvage** (2) 2¼" x 42" strips from each Cut 1 strip of each in half	(57) 2¼" x 42" strips	(54) 2¼" x 21" strips
Background 6½ yds	(22) 2¼" x 42" strips Cut 18 strips in half	(4) 2¼" x 42" strips	(36) 2¼" x 21" strips
Cut Block B and *Outside Border Later*	**Framing Border** (8) 4" x 42" strips		
Binding – 1 yd	(11) 3" x 42" strips		
Backing – 8¼ yds	3 equal pieces		
Batting	Double 94" x 118" Queen 98" x 120"		

King

Approximate Size 113" x 113"
25 A Blocks – 24 B Blocks
Total of Blocks 49
Choose 100% cotton fabric, at least 42" wide.

Terry Albers

Scrap Chain Example

Scrap chains in dark country prints stand out against a bright background in this king size quilt. Machine quilting in large free motion loops, done with a professional quilting machine, is well suited to this large size quilt.

Purchase Yardage	Cut Strips, then…	...Separate Into Two Groups	

Three Color Chain

Purchase Yardage	Cut Strips, then…	Blocks	Seminole Border
	Cut strips selvage to selvage		
Color 1 – 2⅛ yds	(30) 2¼" x 42" strips Cut 7 strips in half	(13) 2¼" x 42" strips (13) 2¼" x 21" strips	(10) 2¼" x 42" strips
Color 2 – 3⅛ yds	(46) 2¼" x 42" strips Cut 12 strips in half	(24) 2¼" x 42" strips (24) 2¼" x 21" strips	(10) 2¼" x 42" strips
Color 3 – 2¾ yds	(40) 2¼" x 42" strips Cut 10 strips in half	(20) 2¼" x 42" strips (20) 2¼" x 21" strips	(10) 2¼" x 42" strips
Background 7¼ yds	(26) 2¼" x 42" strips Cut 2 strips in half	(4) 2¼" x 42" strips (4) 2¼" x 21" strips	(20) 2¼" x 42" strips
Cut Block B and *Outside Border Later*	**Framing Border** (9) 4" x 42" strips		
Binding – 1 yd	(11) 3" x 42" strips		
Backing – 10 yds	3 equal pieces		
Batting	120" x 120"		

Yankee Chain

Purchase Yardage	Cut Strips, then…	Blocks	Seminole Border
	Cut strips selvage to selvage		
40 Different Fabrics	(2) 2¼" x 42" strips from each Cut one of each in half	(37) 2¼" x 42" strips (37) 2¼" x 21" strips	(40) 2¼" x 21" strips
Dominant Chain Fabric 2¾ yds	(40) 2¼" x 42" strips Cut 20 strips in half	(20) 2¼" x 42" strips (20) 2¼" x 21" strips	(20) 2¼" x 21" strips
Background 7¼ yds	(26) 2¼" x 42" strips Cut 22 strips in half	(4) 2¼" x 42" strips (4) 2¼" x 21" strips	(40) 2¼" x 21" strips
Cut Block B and *Outside Border Later*	**Framing Border** (9) 4" x 42" strips		
Binding – 1 yd	(11) 3" x 42" strips		
Backing – 10 yds	3 equal pieces		
Batting	120" x 120"		

Scrap Chain

Purchase Yardage	Cut Strips, then…	Blocks	Seminole Border
	Cut strips selvage to selvage		
60 Different Fabrics	(2) 2¼" x 42" strips from each Cut 1 strip of each in half	(57) 2¼" x 42" strips (57) 2¼" x 21" strips	(60) 2¼" x 21" strips
Background 7¼ yds	(26) 2¼" x 42" strips Cut 2 strips in half	(4) 2¼" x 42" strips (4) 2¼" x 21" strips	(40) 2¼" x 21" strips
Cut Block B and *Outside Border Later*	**Framing Border** (9) 4" x 42" strips		
Binding – 1 yd	(11) 3" x 42" strips		
Backing – 10 yds	3 equal pieces		
Batting	120" x 120"		

Cutting & Sewing Techniques

Cutting 2¼" Strips

Use a 6" x 24" ruler, a large size rotary cutter with a sharp blade, and a gridded cutting mat. Use the mat's grid lines and the ruler's lines to ensure straight cuts. Cut strips from selvage to selvage. Yardage requirements are based on fabric at least 42" wide. If fabric is wider than 42", strips do not need to be trimmed back to 42".

1. Fold the fabric in half, and place on the mat with the fold at the top.

2. Line up the edge of the fabric on the gridded cutting mat with the left edge extended slightly to the left of zero. Reverse this procedure if you are left-handed.

3. Line up the 6" x 24" ruler on zero. Spread the fingers of your left hand to hold the ruler firmly. With the rotary cutter in your right hand, begin cutting with the blade against the ruler. Put all your strength into the rotary cutter as you cut away from you, and straighten the edge.

4. Lift, and move the ruler until it lines up with the 2¼" lines on the grid and cut. Open and check to see that it is straight.

5. For cutting multiple 2¼" strips, lift, and move the ruler until it lines up with the 4½" lines on the grid. Continue across the mat, cutting every 2¼". Sliver trim selvages.

6. After cutting a number of strips, turn mat, and cut them into the necessary length according to the cutting chart for the size quilt you are making.

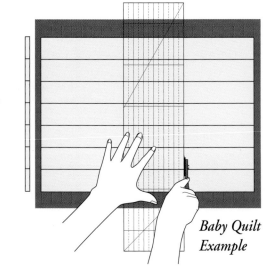

Baby Quilt Example

The length of the strip changes for each size quilt. The longer the strip, the larger the quilt.

Quilt Size	Length of Strips	Cutting Instructions
Baby/Wallhanging	2¼" x 14"	Layer cut at 14". The folded piece is 14".
Lap	2¼" x 21"	Sliver trim on the fold.
Twin	2¼" x 24"	Open strip and cut at 24". The remainder is 18".
Double/Queen	2¼" x 42"	Leave strips selvage to selvage.
King	2¼" x 42"	Leave strips selvage to selvage.
	+2¼" x 21"	Sliver trim on the fold.

Sewing

Use an accurate ¼" seam. A fabric guide placed ¼" from the needle is helpful when sewing the strips into strip sets. Use 15 stitches per inch, or a setting of #2 on machines with stitch selections from 1 to 4.

Assembly-Line Sewing

Save time and thread when sewing several paired pieces by butting them one after another without cutting the thread or removing them from the machine. Use a stiletto to hold your seams flat as you sew over them.

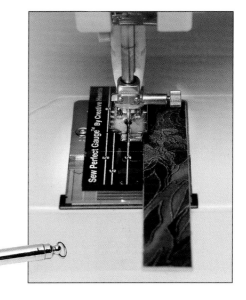

Pressing

It is important to **follow the pressing directions** when sewing this quilt. Seams will then butt together, making the quilt construction easier and the finished top lay flatter. Illustrations show the directions the seams are to be pressed.

Use a gridded pressing mat or a gridded ironing board cover. Place strips or pieces on the gridded lines as indicated by the instructions. Set the seam by placing the iron on the just sewn stitches. Lift open and press again, directing the seams under the top piece. Make certain to press out all folds.

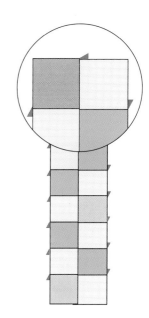

Overview of Two Blocks

Block A

Block A has seven rows.

All Block A's are sewn before starting Block B.

One strip is needed for each piece in the block, or a total of forty-nine 2¼" strips. The King Quilt is the exception, requiring 1½ strips per row.

Rows   1   2   3   4   5   6   7

Block B

Block B has five rows.

Block B Background is cut using measurements from Block A.

One strip is needed for each piece in the block, or a total of twelve 2¼" strips, plus Background.
The King Quilt is the exception, requiring 1½ strips per row.

Rows   1   2   3   4   5

Quilt Size	A Blocks	B Blocks
Baby/Wallhanging	5	4
Lap Robe	8	7
Twin	9	9
Double/Queen	18	17
King	25	24

Three Color Chain

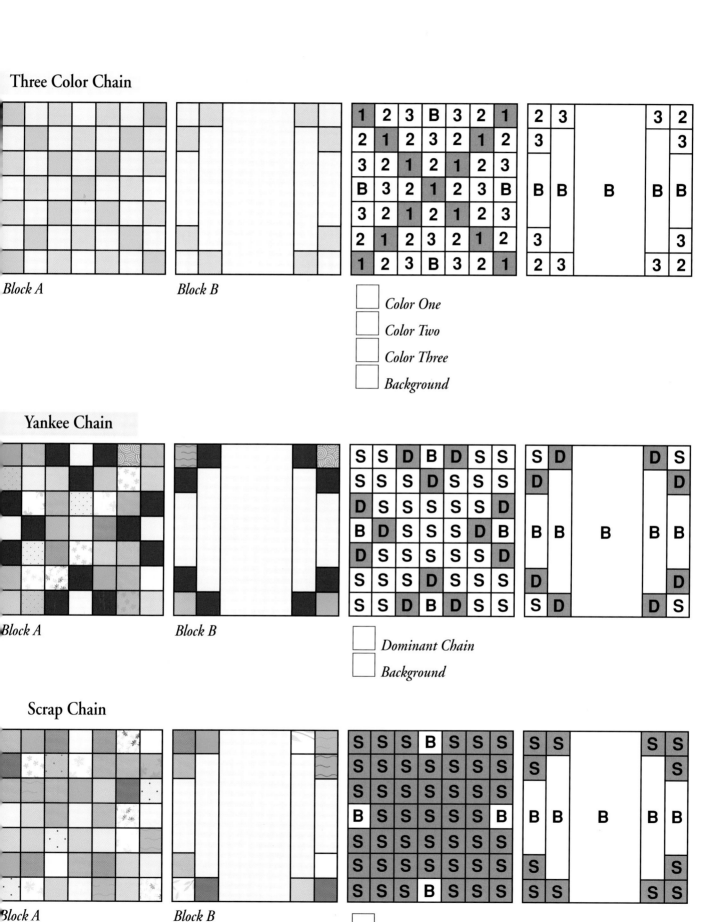

Block A

Block B

1	2	3	B	3	2	1
2	1	2	3	2	1	2
3	2	1	2	1	2	3
B	3	2	1	2	3	B
3	2	1	2	1	2	3
2	1	2	3	2	1	2
1	2	3	B	3	2	1

2	3				3	2
3						3
B	B		B		B	B
3						3
2	3				3	2

☐ *Color One*
☐ *Color Two*
☐ *Color Three*
☐ *Background*

Yankee Chain

Block A

Block B

S	S	D	B	D	S	S
S	S	S	D	S	S	S
D	S	S	S	S	S	D
B	D	S	S	S	D	B
D	S	S	S	S	S	D
S	S	S	D	S	S	S
S	S	D	B	D	S	S

S	D				D	S
D						D
B	B		B		B	B
D						D
S	D				D	S

☐ *Dominant Chain*
☐ *Background*

Scrap Chain

Block A

Block B

S	S	S	B	S	S	S
S	S	S	S	S	S	S
S	S	S	S	S	S	S
B	S	S	S	S	S	B
S	S	S	S	S	S	S
S	S	S	S	S	S	S
S	S	S	B	S	S	S

S	S				S	S
S						S
B	B		B		B	B
S						S
S	S				S	S

☐ *Background*

Arranging Strips for Block A

1. Begin with Row 7.

2. Fold strips in fourths.

3. On the cutting mat, lay seven strips next to each other.

4. Leave approximately 2" of Row 7 showing and line up the next seven strips for Row 6.

5. Continue until you have all seven rows laid out.

6. Review your strip placement for each row.

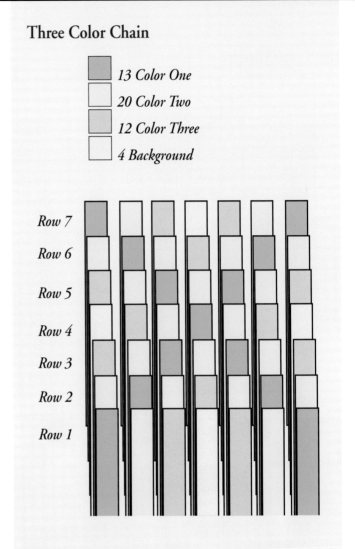

Three Color Chain

13 Color One
20 Color Two
12 Color Three
4 Background

Row 7
Row 6
Row 5
Row 4
Row 3
Row 2
Row 1

Arranging Strips for Block B

Get an idea of what Block B will look like and check color placement.

1. Fold your background fabric into an approximate 13" square.

2. Fold the twelve strips of Block B into approximately 2" squares.

3. Lay on top of the background fabric in the corners according to the color placement.

4. Place this block layout next to Block A to check the color placement.

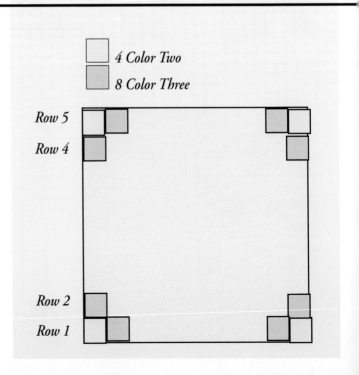

4 Color Two
8 Color Three

Row 5
Row 4
Row 2
Row 1

Yankee Chain

Scrap Chain

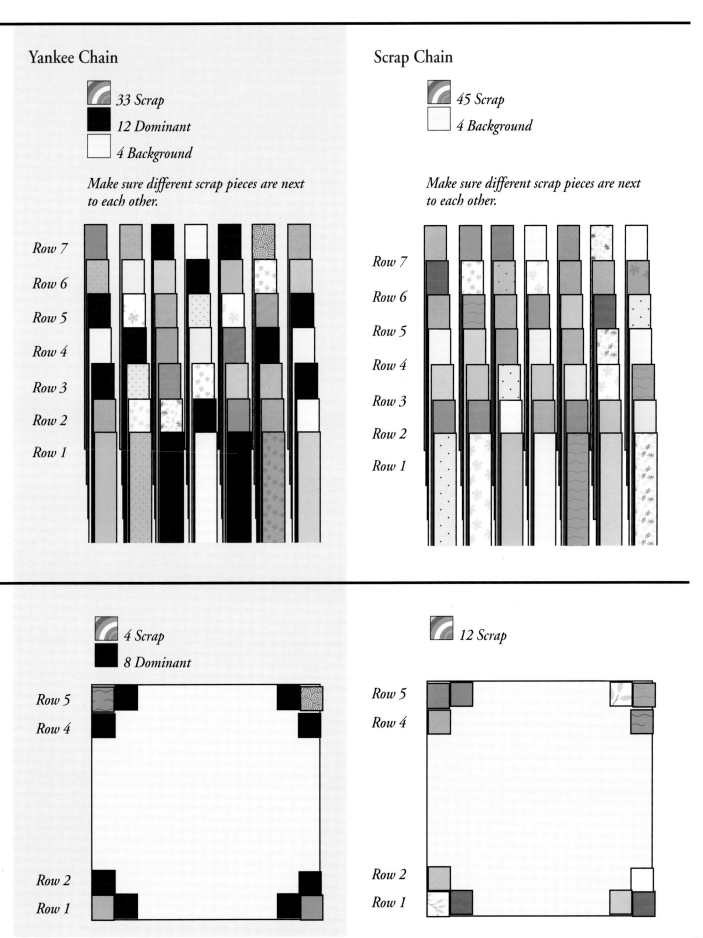

Making Safety Pin Labels

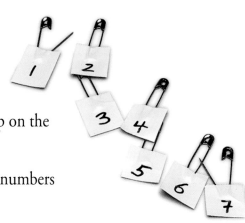

1. Count out seven safety pins.

2. Tear off 1" pieces of masking tape, and wrap on the end of each safety pin.

3. With a fine point permanent marker, write numbers 1 through 7 on the masking tape.

Maribeth Maher

Scrap Quilt

Scrappy reds and blues in cheerful prints contrast with a background fabric in a soft blue. Masculine fabrics make this a good quilt for a boy.

Making Block A

Sewing the Strip Sets for all Seven Rows

1. Place the cutting mat with strip layout for Block A to the left of sewing machine.

2. Cover up Rows 2 through 7 with 16" Square Up ruler.

Three Color Chain Example

Row 7
Row 6
Row 5
Row 4
Row 3
Row 2
Row 1

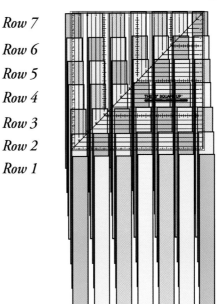

3. Pull off strips for Row 1.

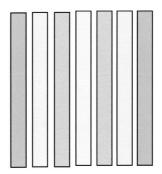

Making Row 1

1. Check your strips.

2. Flip the second strip onto the first strip, right sides together. Flip the fourth strip onto the third strip. Flip the sixth strip onto the fifth strip. There will be one strip left over.

Three Color Chain

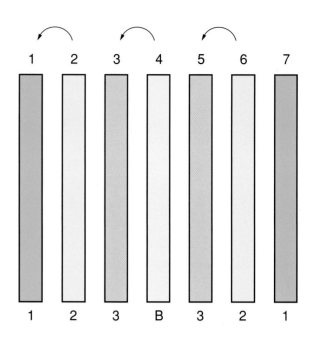

Yankee Chain

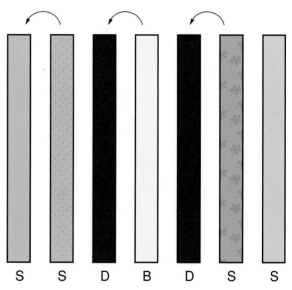

Scrap Chain

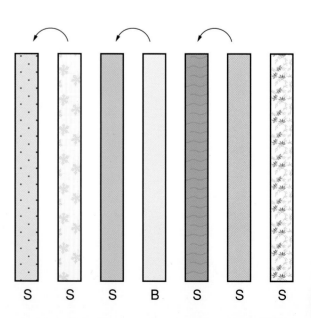

3. Stack the pairs with strips 1/2 on top.

4. Match the top edges, and assembly-line sew the length of each pair.

   All three variations are sewn the same way.

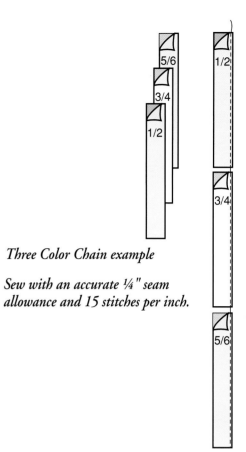

Three Color Chain example

Sew with an accurate ¼" seam allowance and 15 stitches per inch.

5. Clip connecting threads. Place pairs back in their original strip layout order.

6. Flip pair 3/4 onto pair 1/2. Flip strip 7 onto pair 5/6.

7. Match the top edges, and assembly-line sew.

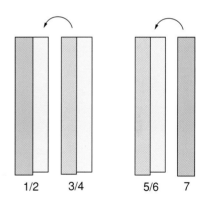

8. Sew the remaining seam of Row 1.

9. Place Row 1 labeled safety pin in the first sewn strip.

10. Measure strip width. It should be approximately 12¾" wide.

11. Set aside.

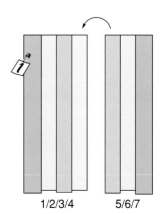

Making Row 2

1. Move the 16" Square Up ruler on the strip layout to expose Row 2. Check your strips.

2. Place #2 labeled safety pin in the first strip.

3. Assembly-line sew.

4. Set aside.

Three Color Chain

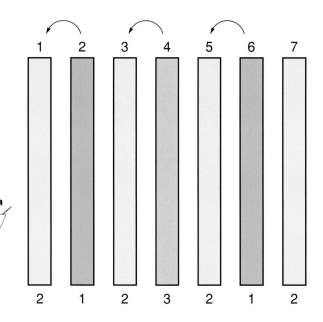

Yankee Chain

Scrap Chain

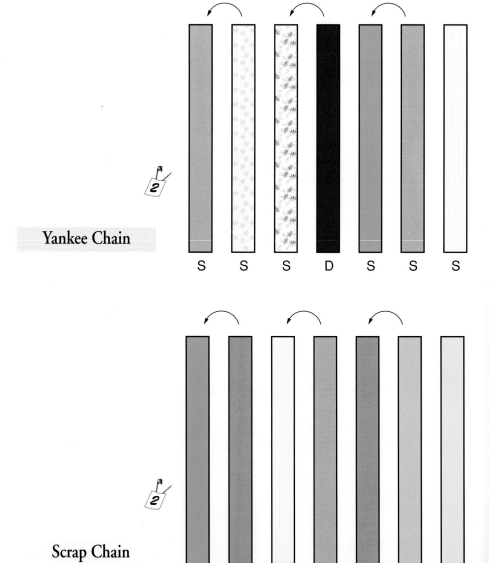

Making Row 3

1. Move the 16" Square Up ruler on the strip layout to expose Row 3. Check your strips.

2. Place #3 labeled safety pin in the first strip.

3. Assembly-line sew.

4. Set aside.

Three Color Chain

Yankee Chain

Scrap Chain

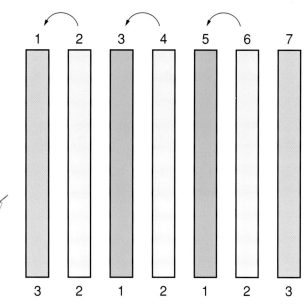
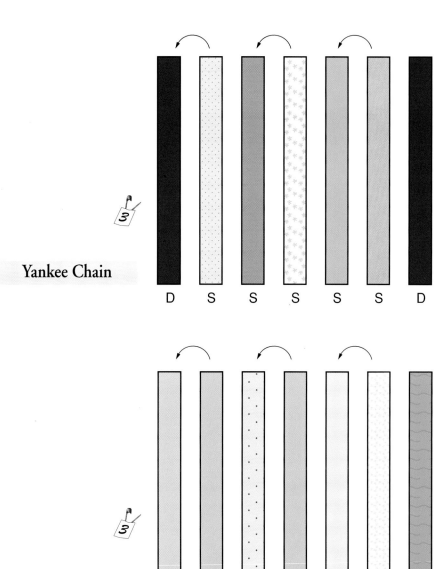

Making Row 4

1. Move the 16" Square Up ruler on the strip layout to expose Row 4. Check your strips.

2. Place #4 labeled safety pin in the first strip.

3. Assembly-line sew.

4. Set aside.

Three Color Chain

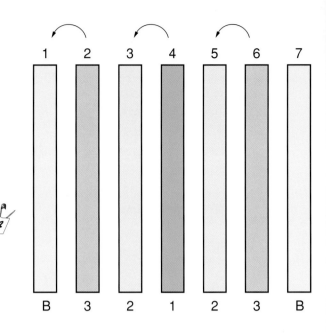

Yankee Chain

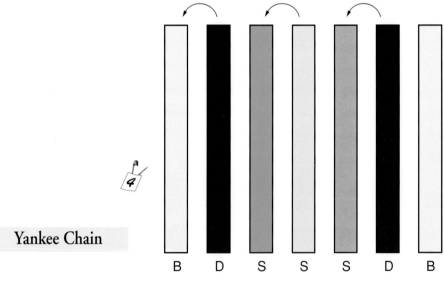

Scrap Chain

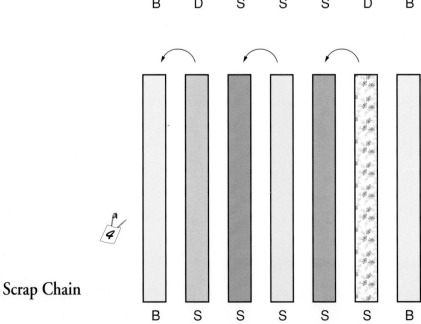

Making Row 5

1. Move the 16" Square Up ruler on the strip layout to expose Row 5. Check your strips.

2. Place #5 labeled safety pin in the first strip.

3. Assembly-line sew.

4. Set aside.

Three Color Chain

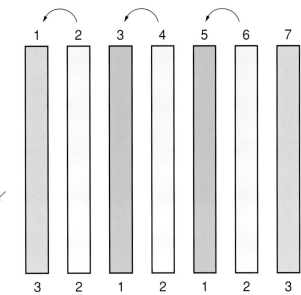

Yankee Chain

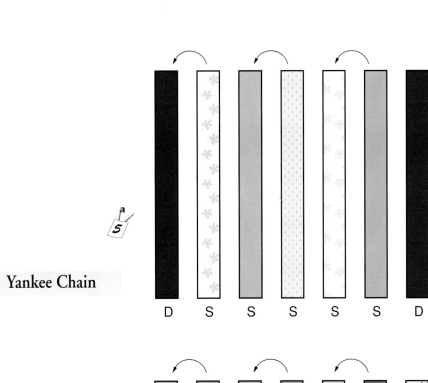

Scrap Chain

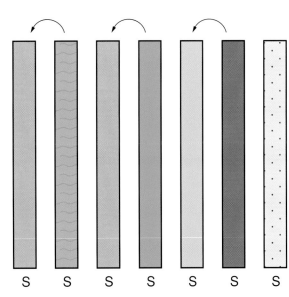

Making Row 6

1. Move the 16" Square Up ruler on the strip layout to expose Row 6. Check your strips.

2. Place #6 labeled safety pin in the first strip.

3. Assembly-line sew.

4. Set aside.

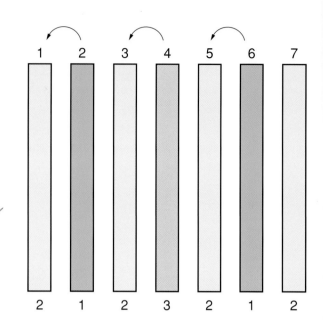

Three Color Chain

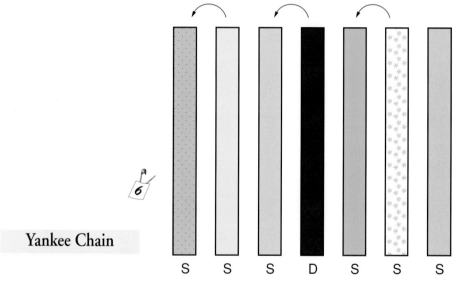

Yankee Chain

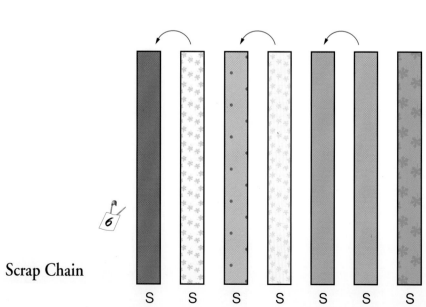

Scrap Chain

Making Row 7

1. Move the 16" Square Up ruler away. Check your strips.

2. Place #7 labeled safety pin in the first strip.

3. Assembly-line sew.

4. Set aside.

Three Color Chain

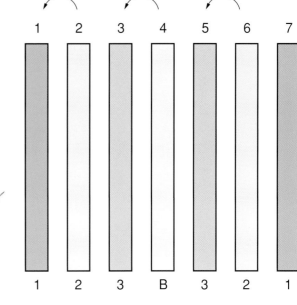

Yankee Chain

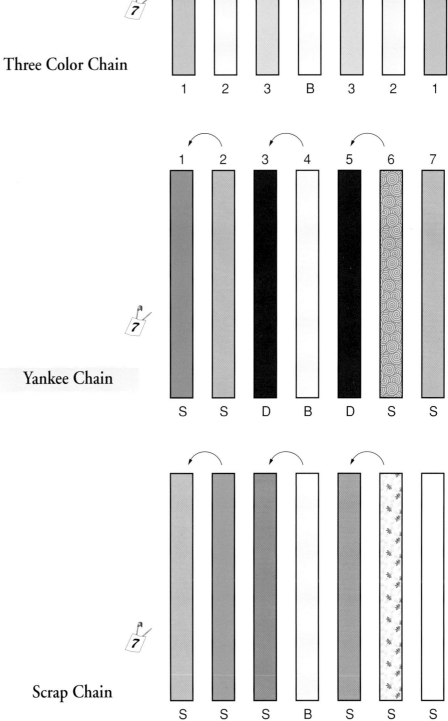

Scrap Chain

Pressing the Strip Sets for all Rows

Follow this method of pressing to eliminate bowed strips and tucks at the seams, and to make seams butt together.

1. Turn pressing mat to vertical position.

2. Press and set all seams on Strip Set 1.

3. Lay Strip Set One, wrong side up, on the pressing mat with the first sewn strip at the right and lined up with the grid. **Do not remove safety pin.** While gently pulling the last strip with one hand, press seams away from the first strip. Press right side of strip set.

4. Press odd strip sets 3, 5, and 7 in same manner.

5. Press seams on remaining even numbered strip sets 2, 4, and 6 toward first strip.

Always keep the first sewn strip lined up with the pressing mat grid.

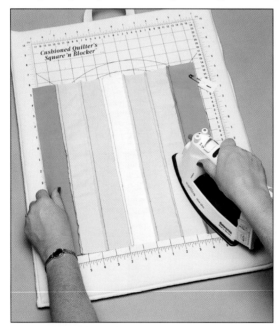

Seams on odd numbered strip sets are pressed away from first strip.

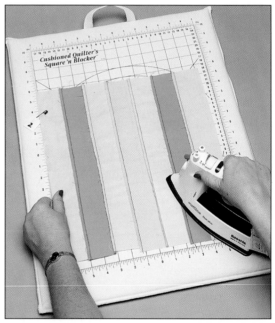

Seams on even numbered strip sets are pressed toward first strip.

6. Square the uneven ends of all strip sets.

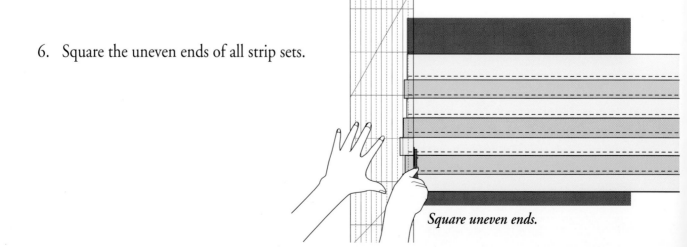

Square uneven ends.

Layer Cutting Strip Sets 1 & 2

1. Place Strip Set 1, right side up, on the cutting mat with the first sewn strip at the top along one grid line. Place seams down.

2. Line up left edge slightly to the left of zero.

3. Place Strip Set 2, right sides together to Strip Set 1. Place with seams up and first strip across the top.

4. Line up the straight edges and left ends. **Lock seams by pushing them together with your fingers.** Square the left end on zero.

5. Find the 2¼" line on your ruler. Mark with masking tape if necessary.

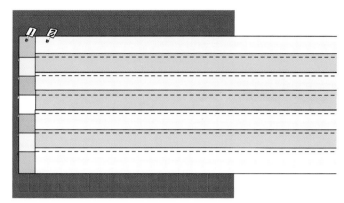

Strip Set One on bottom, seams down.
Strip Set Two on top, seams up.
They should be the same width. If they are not, one strip may be too wide or too narrow, or may need repressing.

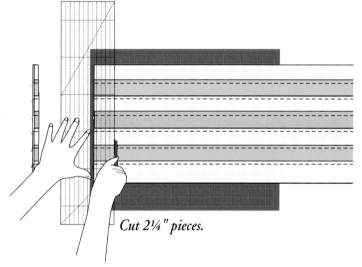

6. Cut 2¼" layered pieces according to the number of Block A's needed for your size quilt. Lift and move the ruler as you cut.

Cut 2¼" pieces.

7. Stack pairs with Row 2 on top and place on another ruler for easy transporting to the sewing machine.

Quilt Size	Pairs
Baby/Wallhanging	5
Lap Robe	8
Twin	9
Double/Queen	18
King	25

Sewing Rows 1 & 2

1. Assembly-line sew with Row 2 on top. Use the stiletto to hold the seams flat as you sew over them. The top seam butts into the seam underneath.

2. Clip threads.

3. Drop sewn pieces on the pressing mat with Row 1 on top. Line up with grid. Set the seam.

4. Lift open and press flat, seam toward Row 1. Stack. Set aside.

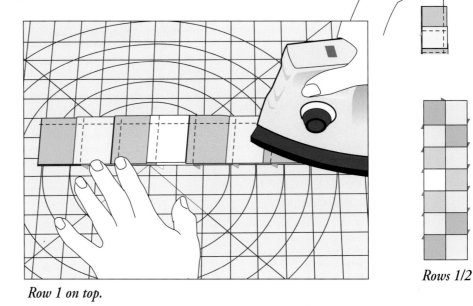

Row 2 on top.

Rows 1/2

Row 1 on top.

Layer Cutting and Sewing Strip Sets 3 & 4

1. Place Strip Set 3 on the bottom with seams down. Place Strip Set 4 on top right sides together with seams up. Place first strips across the top. Lock seams.

2. Square left end. Cut 2¼" pieces for your size quilt and stack.

3. Assembly-line sew with Row 4 on top.

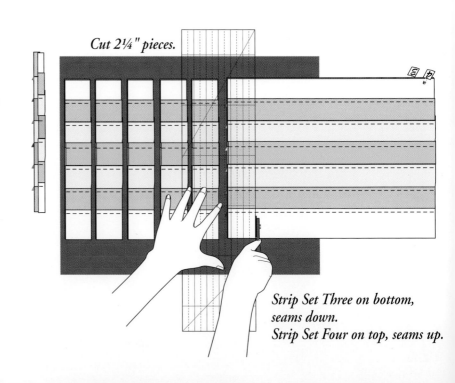

Cut 2¼" pieces.

Strip Set Three on bottom, seams down.
Strip Set Four on top, seams up.

4. Clip threads.

5. Drop the sewn pieces on the pressing mat with Row 3 on top. Set the seams.

6. Lift open, and press seam toward Row 3.

7. Stack next to previously sewn rows.

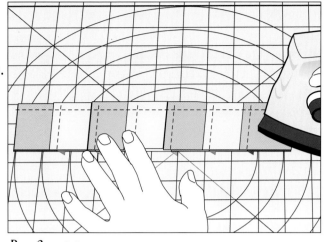

Row 3 on top.

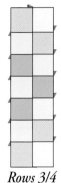

Rows 3/4

Layer Cutting and Sewing Strip Sets 5 & 6

1. Place Strip Set 5 on the bottom with seams down. Place Strip Set 6 on top right sides together with seams up. Place first strips across the top. Lock seams.

2. Square left end. Cut 2¼" pieces for your size quilt and stack.

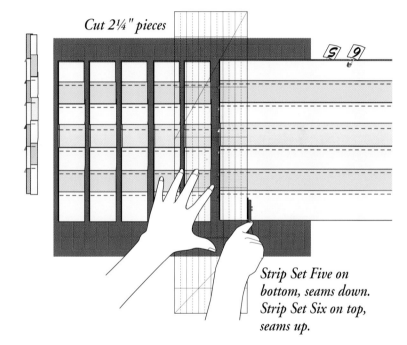

Cut 2¼" pieces

Strip Set Five on bottom, seams down. Strip Set Six on top, seams up.

3. Assembly-line sew with Row 6 on top.

4. Clip threads.

5. Drop the sewn pieces on the pressing mat with Row 6 on top. Set the seams.

6. Lift open, and press seam toward Row 6.

7. Stack next to previously sewn rows.

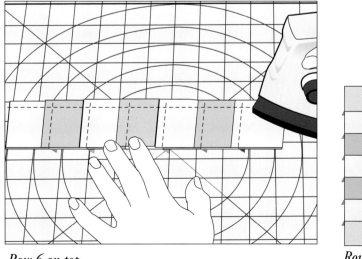

Row 6 on top.

Rows 5/6

Cutting Strip Set 7

1. Lay Strip Set 7 right side up on the cutting mat with the first sewn strip at the top. Line up the strip with the grid. Place seams down. Square left end.

2. Cut 2¼" pieces according to the number of Block A's needed for your size quilt.

3. Stack next to the previously sewn rows.

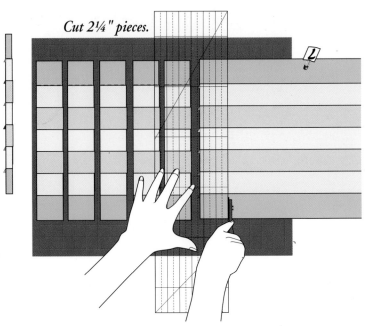

Cut 2¼" pieces.

Sewing the Remaining Seams of Block A

1. Flip the second set of sewn rows onto the first set. Roll top row back, fingermatch seams, and hold together as you stitch over them. Seams should butt together. Assembly-line sew.

2. With Row 1/2 on top, set seam and press toward Row 2.

3. Flip the last single row onto the third set of sewn rows. Butt seams and assembly-line sew.

4. With Row 7 on top, set seam and press toward Row 7.

5. Flip right half of block onto left half. Butt seams and assembly-line sew the two halves together.

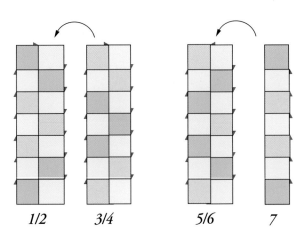

1/2   3/4   5/6   7

Vertical seams are pressed away from center.

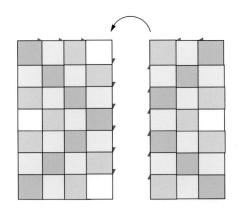

6. From wrong side, press vertical seams of Block A away from center.

   Hang half of the block off the pressing mat. Press one half at a time.

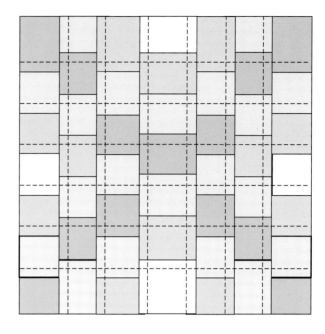

7. Press from the right side.

8. If necessary, sliver trim any uneven edges.

9. Measure the finished size of several Block A's for an average measurement.

   Write your measurement here

   [ ]

   Approx. measurement 12¾"

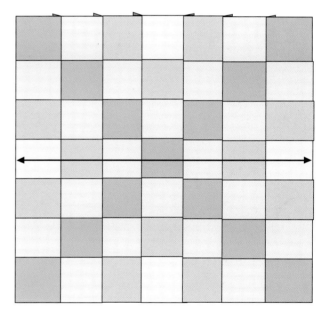

Making Block B

Block B has five rows.
Block B Background strips are cut using measurements from your Block A.

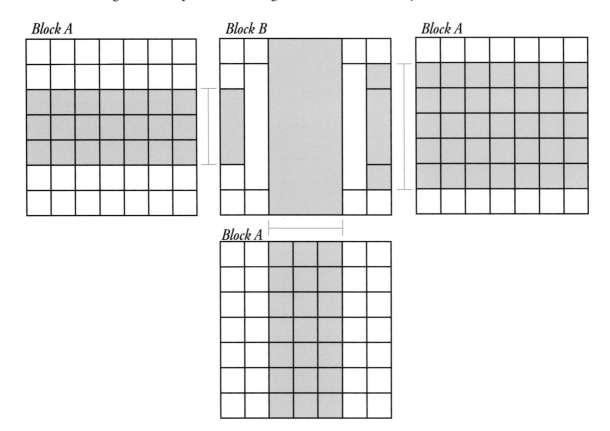

Block A

Block B

Block A

Block A

Cutting the Background Fabric for Rows 1 & 5

1. From the wrong side of Block A, fold under the two outside rows on each side.

2. Measure several different blocks to find the average combined width of Rows 3/4/5 including seam allowances.

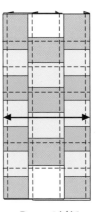

Rows 3/4/5

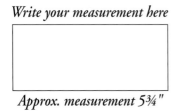

Write your measurement here

Approx. measurement 5¾"

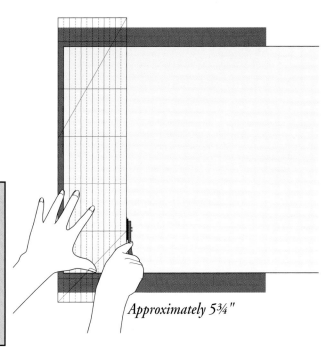

3. Cut background strips selvage to selvage in that measurement.

Quilt Size	Strips
Baby/Wallhanging	1 strip
Lap Robe	1 strip
Twin	2 strips
Double/Queen	2 strips
King	3 strips

Approximately 5¾"

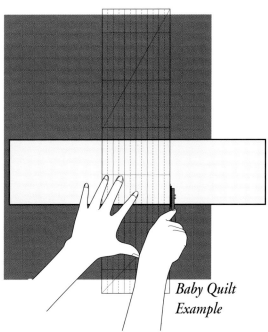

4. Cut into two pieces for Rows 1 and 5.

Baby Quilt Example

Quilt Size	Rows 1 & 5
Baby/Wallhanging	(2) 14" lengths
Lap Robe	(2) 21" lengths
Twin	(2) 24" lengths
Double/Queen	(2) selvage to selvage lengths
King	(2) selvage to selvage lengths
	+ (2) 21" lengths

Sewing Strip Sets 1 & 5

1. Lay the strip sets for each row to the left of your sewing machine.

2. Sew the 2¼" strips in pairs.

3. Sew a strip pair to each side of background strips.

4. Place #1 and #5 labeled safety pins in the first sewn strips.

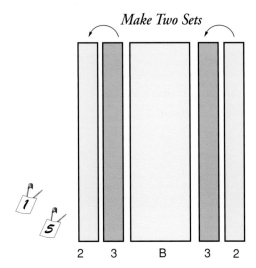

Make Two Sets

Three Color Chain

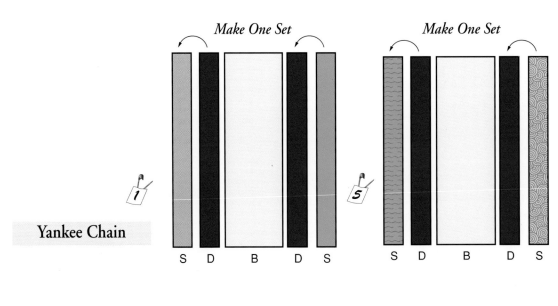

Make One Set   *Make One Set*

Yankee Chain

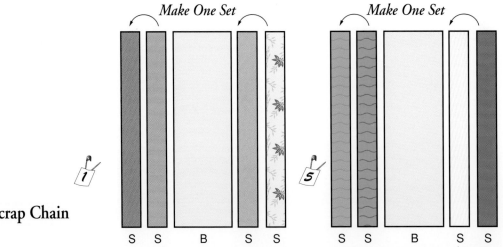

Make One Set   *Make One Set*

Scrap Chain

5. Set seams.

6. Press seams **toward** the first sewn strip on both strip sets.

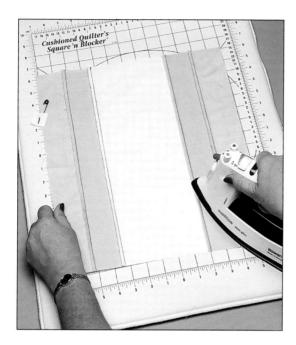 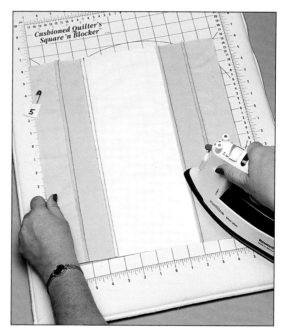

7. Place next to Block A. Make certain strip set fits with Block A.

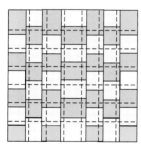 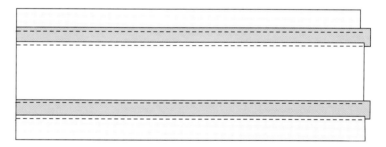

Cutting the Background Fabric for Rows 2 & 4

1. From the wrong side of Block A, fold under the outside row on each side.

2. Measure several different blocks to find the average combined width of Rows 2/3/4/5/6, including seam allowances.

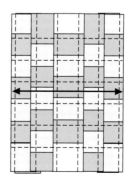

Rows 2/3/4/5/6

Write your measurement here

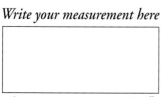

Approx. measurement 9¼"

3. Cut the number of background strips needed in that measurement. Use the grid lines on the gridded mat.

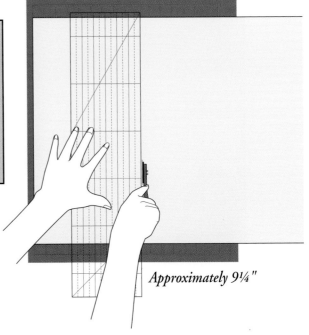

Approximately 9¼″

Quilt Size	Strips
Baby/Wallhanging	1 strip
Lap Robe	1 strip
Twin	2 strips
Double/Queen	2 strips
King	3 strips

4. Cut into two pieces for Rows 2 and 4.

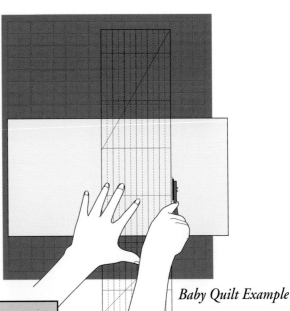

Baby Quilt Example

Quilt Size	Rows 2 & 4
Baby/Wallhanging	(2) 14″ lengths
Lap Robe	(2) 21″ lengths
Twin	(2) 24″ lengths
Double/Queen	(2) selvage to selvage lengths
King	(2) selvage to selvage lengths + (2) 21″ lengths

Sewing Strip Sets 2 & 4

1. Lay the strip sets for each row to the left of your sewing machine.

2. Sew the 2¼" strips to each side of background strips.

3. Place #2 and #4 labeled safety pins in the first sewn strips.

Three Color Chain

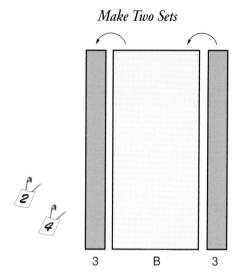

Make Two Sets

Yankee Chain

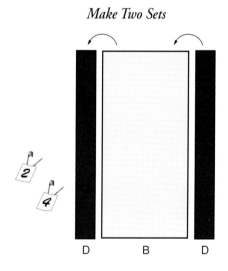

Make Two Sets

Scrap Chain

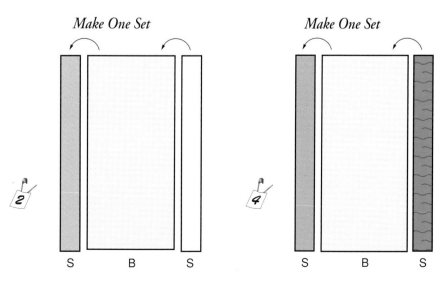

Make One Set   *Make One Set*

4. Set seams.

5. Press seams **away from** the first sewn strip on both strip sets.

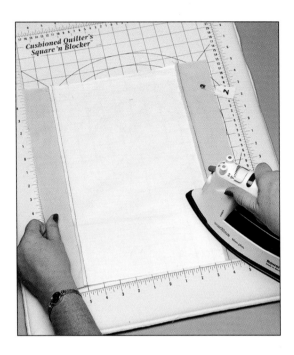 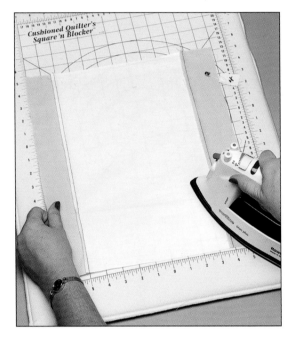

6. Place next to Block A. Make certain strip set fits with Block A.

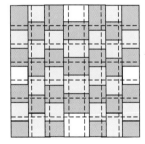 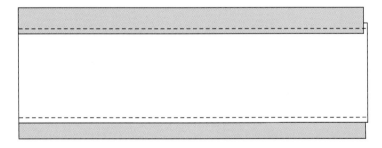

Layer Cutting Strips 1 & 2

1. Place Strip Set 1, right side up, on the cutting mat with the first sewn strip at the top along one grid line. Place seams up.

2. Line up the left edge of the strip set slightly to the left of zero on the cutting mat.

3. Place Strip Set 2, right sides together, to Strip Set 1. Place seams down. Square left end.

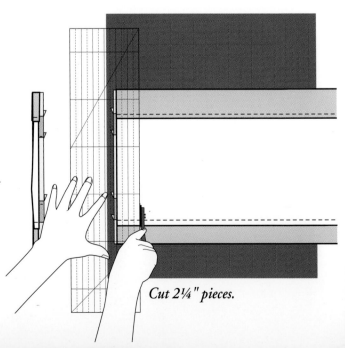

Cut 2¼" pieces.

4. Line up the straight edges and ends. Lock seams.

5. Cut 2¼" layered pieces according to the number of Block B's needed for your size quilt.

Quilt Size	Pairs
Baby/Wallhanging	4
Lap Robe	7
Twin	9
Double/Queen	17
King	24

6. Stack pairs with Row 2 on top. Transport to sewing machine.

7. Assembly-line sew layered pieces.Clip threads.

8. Drop sewn pieces on the pressing mat with
   Row 2 on the top. Set seams. Lift open and press flat,
   seam toward Row 2.

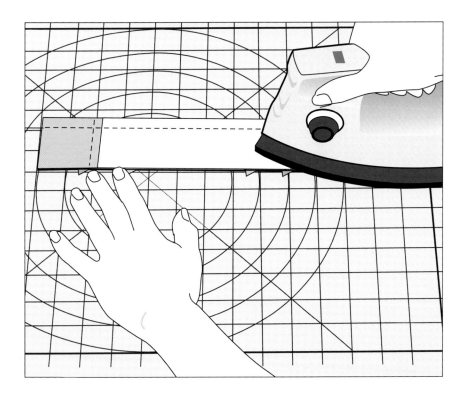

Rows 1/2

Layer Cutting Strip Sets 4 & 5

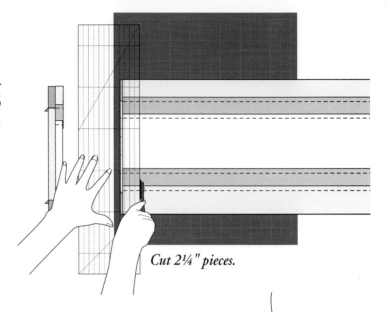

1. Layer cut with Strip Set 4 on the bottom with seams down and Strip Set 5 on top, with seams up. Cut the number needed for your size quilt.

2. Stack with Row 5 on top.

Cut 2¼" pieces.

3. Assembly-line sew. Clip threads.

4. Drop sewn pieces on the pressing mat with Row 4 on the top.

5. Set seams. Lift open and press flat, seam toward Row 4.

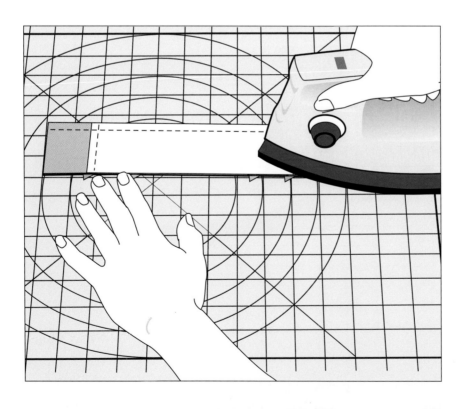

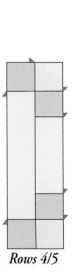

Rows 4/5

Cutting the Background for Row 3

1. Write the measurement of Block A. Refer to page 41.

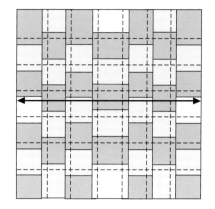

Write your measurement here

Approx. measurement 12¾"

2. Cut strips selvage to selvage the size of your Block A.

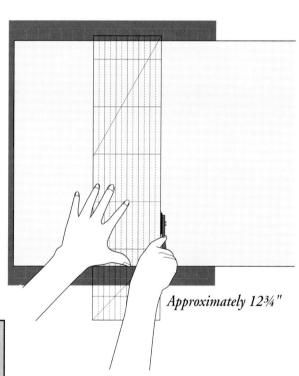

Approximately 12¾"

Quilt Size	Strips
Baby/Wallhanging	1 strip
Lap Robe	1 strip
Twin	2 strips
Double/Queen	3 strips
King	4 strips

3. Refer back to Cutting the Background
    Fabric for Rows 1 & 5, page 42.

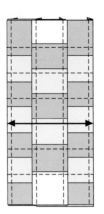

Write your measurement here

Approx. measurement 5¾"

4. Using this measurement, cut the
    background strip(s) for Row 3 into
    the number of Block B's needed
    for your size quilt.

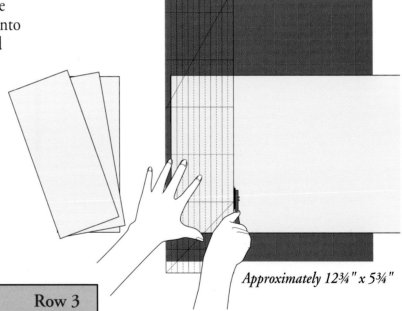

Approximately 12¾" x 5¾"

Quilt Size	Row 3
Baby/Wallhanging	4
Lap Robe	7
Twin	9
Double/Queen	17
King	24

Sewing Block B Together

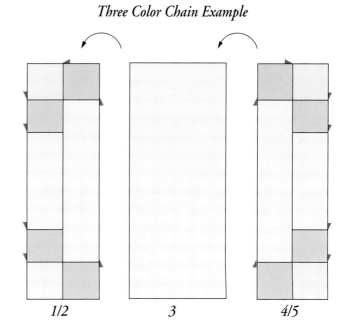

Three Color Chain Example

1. Arrange sewn pieces and background strips.

2. Assembly-line sew the two remaining seams.

   If background strip is shorter than sewn rows, center it before sewing.

   If background strip is longer than sewn rows, trim after sewing.

1/2   3   4/5

3. Set seams. Press seams toward center background strip.

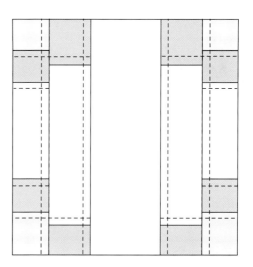

4. Sliver trim block if necessary.

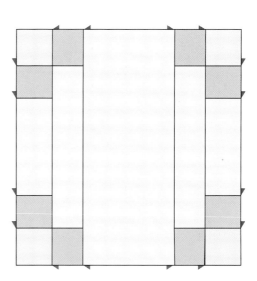

Sewing the Top Together

1. Stack all Block A's with final seams vertical, and Row 1 and Row 7 seams down.

2. Stack all Block B's with final seams vertical and Row 1 and Row 5 seams up.

3. Lay out the rows, alternating the A and B Blocks according to your size quilt.

   Be sure not to turn Blocks! See variation on page 57.

Block A

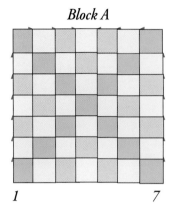

1   *7*

Block B

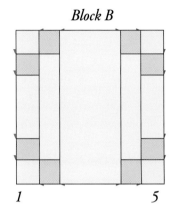

1   *5*

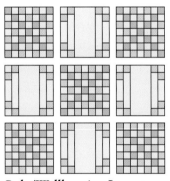

Baby/Wallhanging Layout

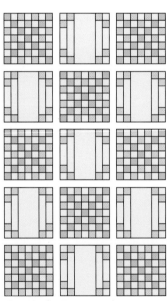

Lap Robe Layout

Twin Layout

Quilt Size	Blocks
Baby/Wallhanging	3 x 3
Lap Robe	3 x 5
Twin	3 x 6
Double/Queen	5 x 7
King	7 x 7

Double/Queen Layout
See variation on page 57.

King Layout

4. Flip the second row onto the first row.

5. Stack the pairs with the top pair on top.

6. Stack the remaining vertical rows from the top to the bottom. The top block should be on the top of the stack each time.

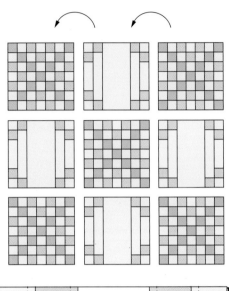

7. Match the outside edges. Carefully lock seams on Rows 1, 2, 6, and 7. Stretch or ease seams to lock.

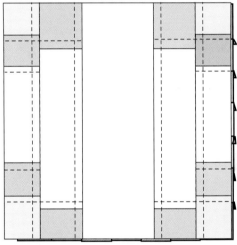

8. Assembly-line sew the first vertical seam. Do not clip the connection threads.

9. Open.

10. Assembly-line sew the third row of blocks. Continue until all the vertical rows are sewn. Do not clip apart.

11. Press just sewn seams toward Block B.

12. Sew the horizontal seams, butting the vertical seams together.

13. Press.

14. Check that corners are square and edges are straight. Trim if necessary.

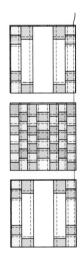
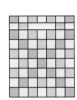
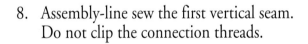

This Double/Queen variation is made by making an extra Block B
and eliminating one Block A. B Blocks are placed on the outside corners of the quilt.

*Double/Queen Variation -
Barbara Crabb*

Adding the Framing Border

Framing Border strips must be 2¼" or 4" wide so the Seminole border will fit. If you choose to use a 2¼" border in place of the designated 4" border, eliminate one single Seminole piece from each side. See page 63.

1. Sew the 2¼" or 4" Frame strips into one long piece. Baby/Wallhanging borders do not need to be pieced together.

2. Cut two pieces the length of the quilt top plus 2".

3. Pin the middle of the strips to the middle of the sides.

4. Leave about 1" of strips beyond quilt. Pin intermittently.

5. With the Frame underneath, sew side strips.

6. Press seams toward Frame.

7. Trim strips even with quilt edges.

8. Cut two pieces from the Frame strip the width of the quilt plus 2".

9. Center and pin strips, leaving about 1" of strips beyond quilt.

10. With Frame underneath, sew top and bottom strips.

11. Trim strips even with quilt edges.

12. Press seams toward Frame.

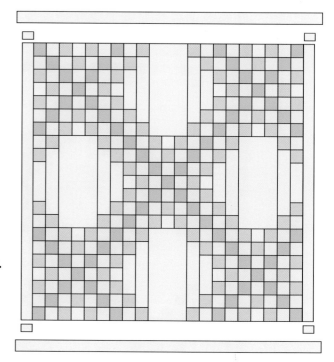

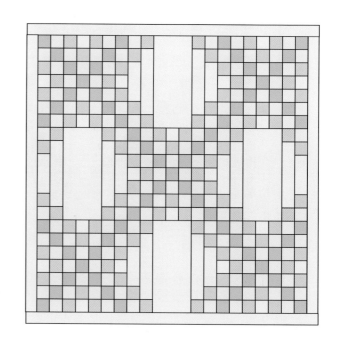

The Seminole Border

The Seminole border is sewn using the 2¼" background strips and the Three Color, Yankee or Scrap strips set aside after cutting.

1. Lay out the number of Seminole Strip Sets according to the pattern and size quilt you are making.

2. Assembly-line sew the strip sets.

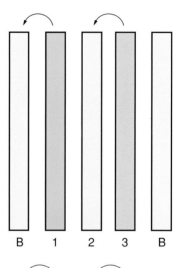

Three Color Chain	Strip Sets
Baby/Wallhanging	(5) 42" strip sets
Lap Robe	(14) 21" strip sets
Twin	(16) 18" strip sets
Double/Queen	(8) 42" strip sets
King	(10) 42" strip sets

Arrange your fabrics in any order that is pleasing to you. In this example, Color 3 is the outside fabric.

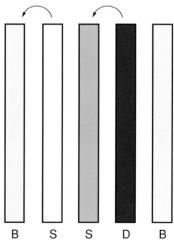

Yankee Chain	Strip Sets
Baby/Wallhanging	(16) 14" strip sets
Lap Robe	(14) 21" strip sets
Twin	(16) 18" strip sets
Double/Queen	(18) 21" strip sets
King	(20) 21" strip sets

In this example, the Dominant color is the outside fabric.

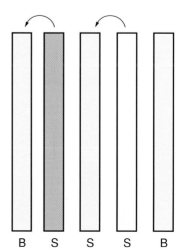

Scrap Chain	Strip Sets
Baby/Wallhanging	(16) 14" strip sets
Lap Robe	(14) 21" strip sets
Twin	(16) 18" strip sets
Double/Queen	(18) 21" strip sets
King	(20) 21" strip sets

3. Press to set each seam on the strip sets.

4. Press seams according to the quilt pattern you are making.

5. Sliver trim to square up the uneven end of each strip set.

Three Color Chain

Baby/Wallhanging - cut one strip set in half. Press half the strip sets in one direction and half in the opposite direction.

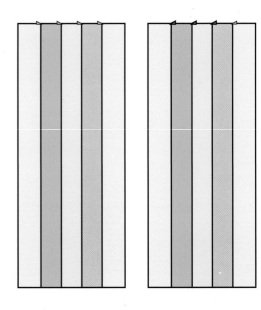

Yankee Chain

Press half the strip sets in one direction and half in the opposite direction.

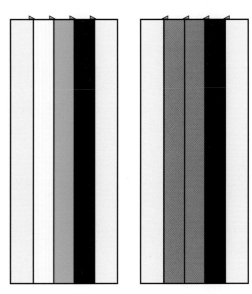

Scrap Chain

Press the seams of all the strip sets in one direction.

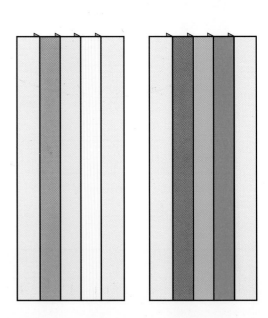

Layer Cutting the Seminole Border Strip Sets

Use the layer cutting technique again but this time stagger the top strip set one strip lower than the first strip set. Seminole pairs will then be ready to sew.

1. Layer the strip sets according to the pattern you are making:

Three Color Chain

Place first strip set right side up, outside color at the bottom, seams down.
Place second strip set one strip lower than previous strip set, right side down.
Outside color at the bottom, seams up.

Yankee Chain

Place first strip set right side up, dominant color at the bottom, seams down.
Place second strip set one strip lower than previous strip set, right side down.
Dominant color at the bottom, seams up.

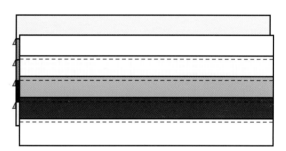

Scrap Chain

Place first strip set right side up, seams down.
Place second strip set one strip lower than previous strip set, right side down, seams up.

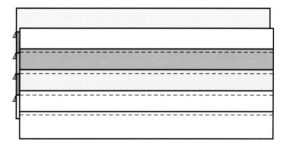

2. Line up the left ends slightly to the left of zero on the cutting mat.

3. Square the left ends by sliver trimming the layered strip sets along the zero line.

4. See chart on page 62 and cut 2¼" Seminole pairs according to the size of your quilt. Stack pairs.

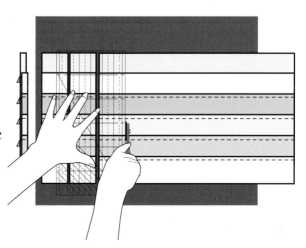

You should get 6 pairs from each 14" strip set, 7 pairs from each 18" strip set, 9 pairs from each 21" strip set, and 18 from each 42" strip set.

Quilt Size	Three Color Pairs	Yankee Pairs	Scrap Pairs
Baby/Wallhanging	38	38	36
Lap Robe	50	50	48
Twin	55	55	53
Double/Queen	70	70	68
King	80	80	78

5. From these cut pairs, count out a **variety** of pairs for the Scrap and Yankee. Three color pairs are all the same. **Set aside** for Borders and Corners.

Quilt Size	Three Color Pairs	Yankee Pairs	Scrap Pairs
Baby/Wallhanging	6	6	4
Lap Robe	8	8	6
Twin	7	7	5
Double/Queen	8	8	6
King	8	8	6

6. Assembly-line sew pairs. Clip apart.

7. Place on pressing mat with seam on the left and the color that will run along the outside of the Seminole border at the bottom.

8. Press to set seam. Lift open and press seam flat toward higher piece.

Top Seminole piece is always one step lower than bottom Seminole piece.

Top is folded on stitching.

Stitching is showing on bottom piece.

Sewing Seminole Pairs into Borders

1. Open set aside pairs into single Seminole pieces.

2. Stack the sewn pairs and a single piece if necessary into four piles according to the size quilt you are making. Each pile makes a side.

Quilt Size	Seminole Pieces
Baby/Wallhanging	(4) piles of 8 pairs
Lap Robe	(2) piles of 13 pairs + 1 (2) piles of 8 pairs + 1
Twin	(2) piles of 16 pairs (2) piles of 8 pairs + 1
Double/Queen	(2) piles of 18 pairs + 1 (2) piles of 13 pairs + 1
King	(4) piles of 18 pairs + 1

Lap Example-Four different piles

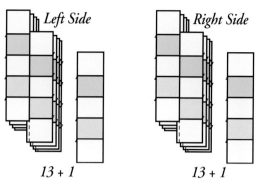

Left Side   *Right Side*

13 + 1   13 + 1

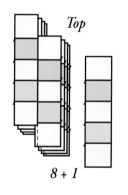 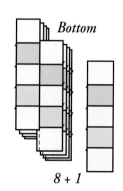

Top   *Bottom*

8 + 1   8 + 1

Yankee Chain

Scrap Chain

"Deal" same pairs into four piles like a deck of cards, so you get a good mix of scraps.

3. **Select one pile and assembly-line sew as many pairs as possible** into groups of fours making certain each new piece is one step lower than the previous one. Mix scrap pairs.

4. Sew groups of fours into the correct length.

5. **Add the single Seminole piece last to the right end.**

6. Press seams all in one direction away from last piece.

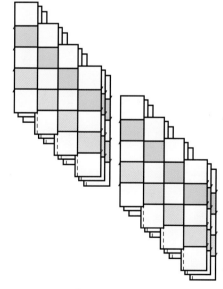

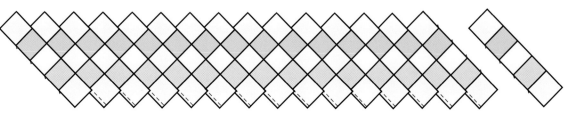

← *Seams*

Making Four Seminole Border Corners

1. Count out Seminole pieces for your particular quilt. Unsew the pieces and arrange as shown. Some parts may be discarded.

2. Press seams as illustrated to butt together.

3. Sew.

4. Do not press.

5. Make four corner sections.

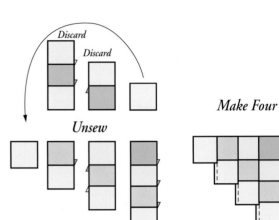

Three Color Chain

Count out three Seminole pieces per corner.

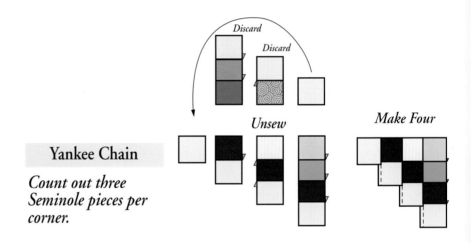

Yankee Chain

Count out three Seminole pieces per corner.

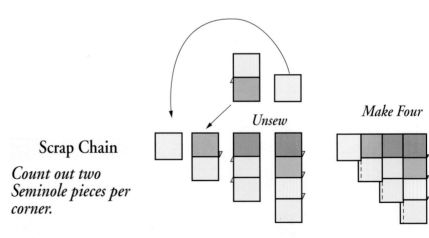

Scrap Chain

Count out two Seminole pieces per corner.

6. Sew a corner section to the left end of each Seminole border.

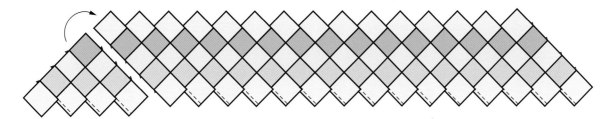

7. Press corner seams in the same direction as the Seminole border.

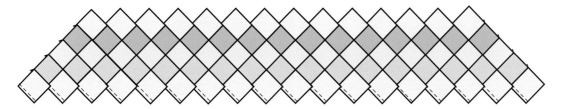

Trimming Seminole Borders

1. Lay one Seminole border strip right side up on the cutting mat.

2. Line up the ⅜" measurement on the 6" x 24" ruler with points of the Seminole border. This will give you a generous ¼" seam. Trim four at a time.

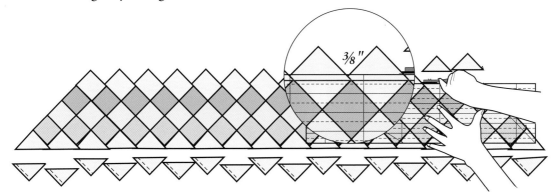

3. Carefully trim both sides of the Seminole strip.

4. Trim remaining three Seminole borders.

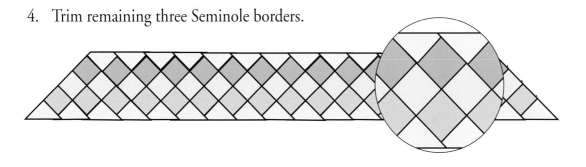

Sewing Seminole Borders to Quilt Top

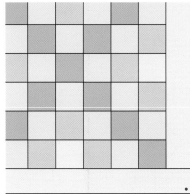

1. On the right side of the quilt top, mark a dot at the ¼" point of each corner and the midpoint of each side.

2. Mark the midpoint of each border.

3. On the wrong side of both border ends, mark a dot at the ¼"point on the seam line between first background square and first colored square.

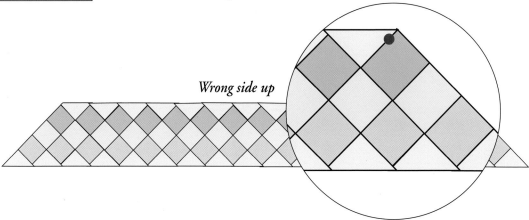

Wrong side up

4. Lay quilt right side up on a flat surface. Pin border midpoint right sides together to quilt midpoint.

Three Color Chain   **Yankee Chain**

Make sure colors flow in the correct direction.

5. Match and pin dot at each border end to the dot at each quilt corner.

6. Pin every triangle. "Pat" Seminole flat to border. Ease or stretch slightly if necessary.

7. Pin the opposite border to the quilt top.

8. Working from the border side, backstitch to the corner dot and then sew to the dot at the other end, and backstitch again. Repeat for opposite side.

   Do not stitch over marked dots into seam allowance. This will cause a tuck at the corner.

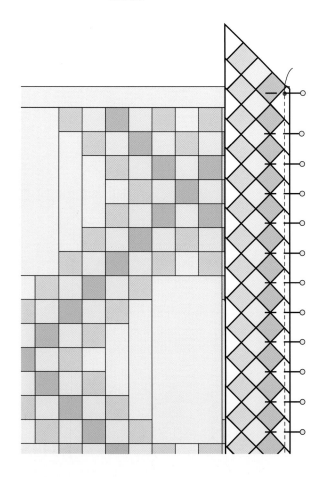

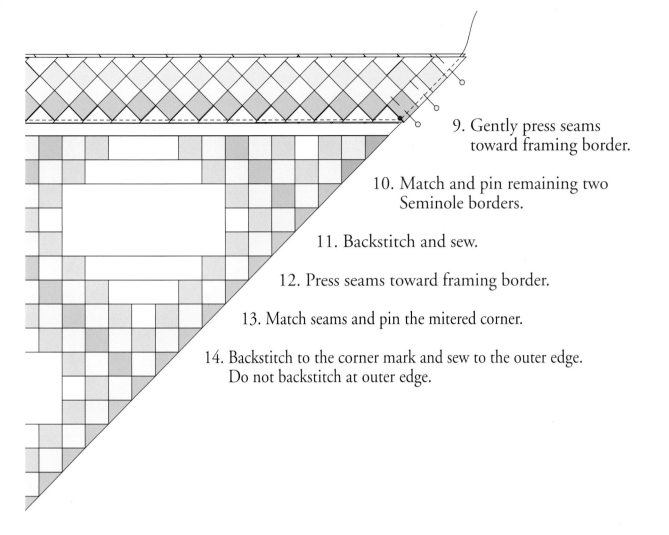

9. Gently press seams toward framing border.

10. Match and pin remaining two Seminole borders.

11. Backstitch and sew.

12. Press seams toward framing border.

13. Match seams and pin the mitered corner.

14. Backstitch to the corner mark and sew to the outer edge. Do not backstitch at outer edge.

15. Press mitered corner seam open. Square corners with Square Up ruler.

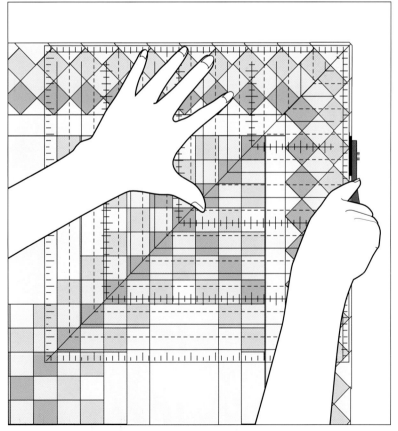

Sewing Outside Border

Before cutting the outside border, lay the quilt top on your bed. Check how much border is needed to get the fit you want. Keep in mind that the quilt will shrink approximately 3" in length and width after machine quilting and even more if you use cotton batting and wash your quilt after it is completed. Adjust the outside border width if necessary.

Quilt Size		Suggested Third Border
Baby/Wallhanging	(6)	2¼" strips
Lap Robe	(7)	4" strips
Twin	(8)	7½" strips
Double	(10)	5½" strips
Queen	(10)	7½" strips
King	(11)	5½" strips

1. Cut background strips for the third border according to the size quilt you are making.

2. Piece border strips.

3. Measure and sew borders to quilt top.

4. Press seams toward outside border.

Finishing the Quilt

Planning your Machine Quilting

Read instructions before proceeding. Choose your favorite method of machine quilting.

Straight line quilting using a walking foot

- Stitch diagonally down the center of at least three of the rows of the chain.
- Stitch in the ditch around each border.
- Diagonal stitch in the ditch through the Seminole border.
- Diagonal stitch the outside border.

Straight line and free motion quilting using a darning foot

- Stitch diagonally down the center of at least three of the rows of the chain.
- Quilt a design in the background area of Block B.
- Quilt a design in the framing border.
- Diagonal stitch in the ditch through the Seminole border.
- Quilt a design in the outside border.

Marking your Quilt for Free Motion Quilting

If you plan to Free Motion machine quilt, mark your quilt top before layering.

1. Choose a continuous line stencil to fit:
   - Block B – 7" x 7" square
   - 2¼" Framing Border – 1½" wide
   - 4" Framing Border – 3" wide
   - Outside Border – 3¼" to 7" wide depending on border width

2. Trace the stencil with a fine line pencil or a water erasable pen. For dark backgrounds use a soapstone pencil or a silver pencil.

Preparing the Backing

1. Refer to your Yardage Chart for the number of pieces to cut the backing into.

2. Fold the backing crosswise and cut into equal pieces. If you custom fitted your quilt, you may need to adjust these measurements.

3. Tear off the selvages. Using a ½" seam, sew the pieces together.

4. Press the seams to one side.

Layering

1. Lay out the backing right side down on a large floor area or table. Tape down on the floor area or clamp onto a table with large binder clips.

2. Place the batting on top and smooth.

3. Lay the quilt top right side up and centered on top of the batting.

4. Straighten the borders in all directions.

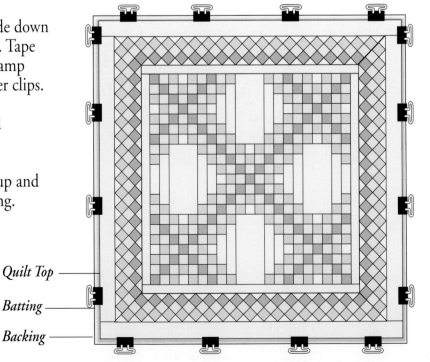

Quilt Top ——

Batting ——

Backing ——

Squaring the Corners and Pinning

1. Place a 16" Square Up ruler in one corner of the quilt along the Seminole border. Adjust the Seminole border so that the seams touch the ruler's edge on two sides.

2. Safety pin around the corner through all layers of the quilt.

3. Repeat for all four corners.

4. Any excess fabric in the quilt top should be evenly distributed.

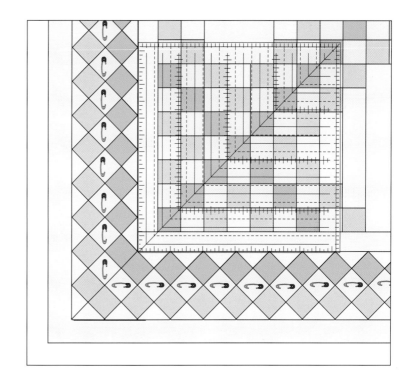

5. Safety pin the entire quilt:
   - Down Rows 2 and 4 of the chain
   - Away from the planned quilting lines of the framing border and the outside border
   - Down the middle row of the Seminole border
   - Away from the quilting lines in the background area of Block B

6. Trim backing and batting to 2" on all sides.

7. Hand baste the three layers of the quilt together ¼" from the raw edge.

Red dots indicate position of safety pins

Stitching the Chain Diagonally

Mark with ¼" masking tape or a Hera Marker.

1. Place a walking foot attachment on your machine.

2. Place invisible thread in the top of your machine. Loosen the top tension.

3. Place regular thread in the bobbin to match the backing.

4. Lengthen your stitch to 8-10 stitches per inch, or a #3 or #4 setting.

5. Roll the quilt tightly from the outside edge diagonally in toward the middle. Hold this roll with quilt clips or Jaws™.

6. Slide this roll into the keyhole of the sewing machine.

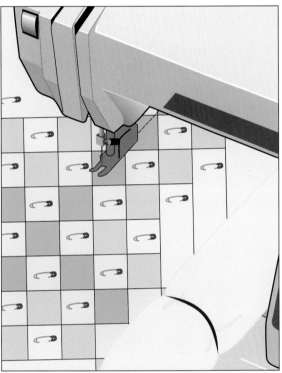

7. Place the needle in the depth of the center row of the chain and pull up the bobbin thread. Lock your thread with ½" of tiny stitches when you begin and end your sewing. Clip the threads.

8. Place your hands flat on both sides of the needle. Keep the quilt area flat and tight. To keep the weight off the quilting area, hold the rest of the quilt on your lap, or place on your shoulder.

9. Sew down the center of the chain either stopping when you come to background fabric or continue sewing diagonally through the background fabric if you are not planning a stencil in the background space. Unroll, roll, and machine quilt all the center rows of each chain.

10. Repeat for the outside rows of each chain.

Stitching in the Ditch

1. Stitch in the ditch around both the framing border and the Seminole border.

2. To anchor each block for free motion quilting, stitch in the ditch down the length and across the width of each row.

3. Stitch in the ditch diagonally through the Seminole border.

Free Motion Quilting

*After stitching in the ditch to anchor your quilt, you are ready to "free motion quilt".
Make a "test sandwich" by tracing the stencil on the background, and then layering it with the
backing and batting. Practice until you become comfortable with the pattern.*

1. Place a darning foot, embroidery foot, or a spring needle on your machine.

2. Drop the feed dogs or cover with a plate. Use a fine needle and a little hole throat plate.

3. Thread the machine on top with invisible or regular thread, and thread to match the backing in the bobbin. Loosen the top tension if using invisible thread.

4. If possible, set your machine to ½ speed.

5. Drop the needle into the traced design and bring up the bobbin thread.

6. Moving the fabric very slowly, take a few tiny stitches to lock them. Snip off the tails of the threads.

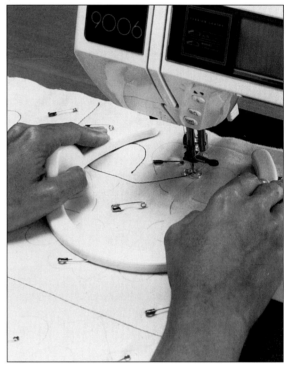

Use a Quilt So Easy™ to help move the quilt.

7. With your eyes watching the outline of the block ahead of the needle, and your fingertips stretching the fabric and acting as a quilting hoop, move the fabric in a steady motion while the machine is running at a constant speed. In place of stretching with your fingers, you can use a Quilt So Easy™ to move the quilt. Keep the top of the quilt in the same position by moving the fabric underneath the needle side to side, and forward and backward.

8. Lock off the tiny stitches and clip the threads at the end of the pattern.

Machine quilting by Lee Codington

Stippling

Stippling is a random type of free motion quilting that adds dimension to this quilt if done in the borders and/or in the remaining background area of Block B after a continuous line design is completed. Use the same machine set-up.

1. Insert the needle at the edge of the background square.

2. Raise the needle, and bring the bobbin thread to the surface. Pull up the slack in the thread. Lock the stitches.

3. Sew a few stitches in one direction, then curve around and back toward the beginning making a loop. Remove safety pins as you sew.

4. Before you reach the point where you began, curve back toward where you started without crossing previously sewn stippling.

5. Continue making loops until you fill the area. Move toward the edge and lock the stitches. Clip loose threads.

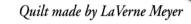

Quilt made by LaVerne Meyer

Machine quilting by Vickie Masse

Binding

1. Assembly-line sew the binding strips into one long strip.

2. Place a walking foot attachment on your sewing machine. Use regular thread on top and in the bobbin to match the binding. Set your machine for 10 stitches per inch, or #3 setting.

3. Press the binding strip in half lengthwise with right sides out.

4. Line up the raw edges of the folded binding with the raw edge of the quilt top at the middle of one side.

5. Begin sewing 4" from the end of the binding using a ⅜" seam allowance.

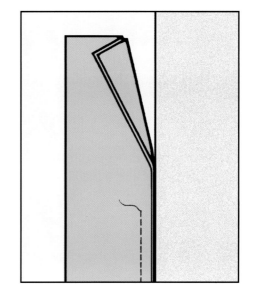

6. At the corner, stop the stitching ⅜" from the edge with the needle in the fabric. Raise the presser foot and turn the quilt to the next side. Put the foot back down.

7. Sew backwards ⅜" to the edge of the binding, raise the foot, and pull the quilt forward slightly.

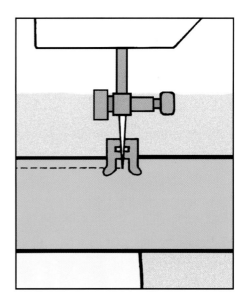

8. Fold the binding strip straight up on the diagonal. Fingerpress in the diagonal fold.

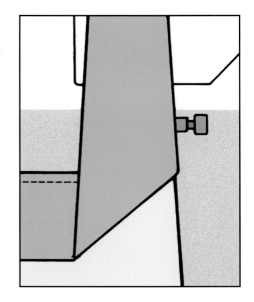

9. Fold the binding strip straight down with the diagonal fold underneath. Line up the top of the fold with the raw edge of the binding underneath.

10. Begin sewing a ⅜" seam from the corner.

11. Continue sewing and mitering the corners around the outside of the quilt.

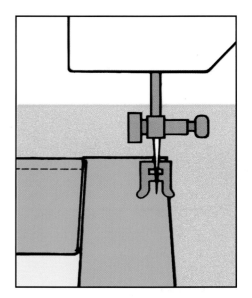

12. Stop sewing 4" from where the ends will overlap.

13. Line up the two ends of binding. Trim the excess with a ½" overlap.

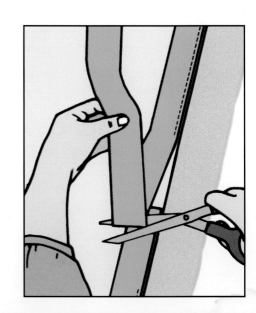

14. Open out the folded ends and pin right sides together. Sew a ¼" seam.

15. Continue to sew the binding in place.

16. Trim the batting and backing up to the raw edges of the binding.

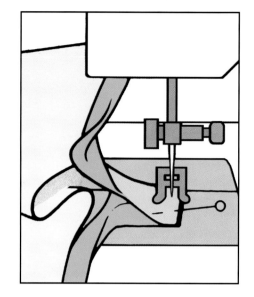

17. Fold the binding to the back side of the quilt. Pin in place so that the folded edge on the binding covers the stitching line. Tuck in the excess fabric at each miter on the diagonal.

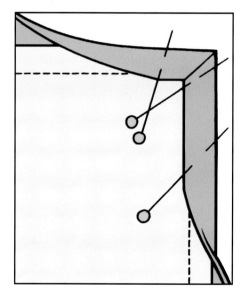

18. Hand slip stitch the folded edge of the binding on the backside.

19. *Optional:* From the right side, "stitch in the ditch" using invisible thread on the right side, and a bobbin thread to match the binding on the back side. Catch the folded edge of the binding on the back side with the stitching.

20. Sew an identification label on the back listing your name, date, and other pertinent information.

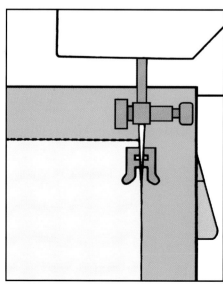

Washing

How to Achieve the Look of an Antique Quilt

Follow these directions whether or not your fabrics were pre-shrunk before quilting.

1. Fill bathtub with warm water.

2. Add quilt soap only if you feel your quilt needs cleaning due to handling or marking during the quilt making process. Use soap specially made for quilts. Follow the directions on the label for the amount of soap to use.

3. Add Retayne™ to the warm water. Retayne™ is a product that will "fix" dyes in commercially purchased cotton fabrics to prevent color bleeding during washing. Estimate the yardage in your quilt and use approximately 1 teaspoon per yard of fabric. Mix thoroughly.

4. Totally submerge your quilt in the bathtub of warm water. Make sure all areas of the quilt get completely wet.

5. If soap was used, rinse thoroughly until all soap is removed.

6. Gently drain quilt by pressing the water out with your hands.
    Handle quilt carefully to eliminate any unnecessary straining of the seams.

7. While still in the bathtub, place quilt in a plastic laundry basket. The basket will make it easier to lift the quilt so it can continue to drain. Remove all excess water from the quilt.

8. Place quilt in the dryer on a medium heat setting along with a couple of big bath towels. The towels will beat the quilt around in the dryer and keep it from bunching up.
    If your quilt is too large for your home dryer, carry it in the basket to a commercial laundry and dry it in a big dryer.

9. Watch closely. Do not dry completely. Remove from dryer while still slightly damp.

10. Lay quilt flat to finish drying.

Acknowledgements

Special Thanks to...

The members of the Sheboygan County Quilters Guild for their assistance and encouragement.

The many quilters all over the state of Wisconsin who tested the instructions.
My friends and former students at Quilt in a Day who also tested the instructions.
My computer technician and husband, Pete.

And to Eleanor Burns, for her ideas and guidance in the writing of this book even though we're 2000 miles part.

Index

Order Information

Quilt in a Day books offer a wide range of techniques that are directed toward a variety of skill levels. If you do not have a quilt shop in your area, you may write or call for a complete catalog and current price list of all books and patterns published by Quilt in a Day®, Inc.

Easy

Quilt in a Day Log Cabin
Irish Chain in a Day
Bits & Pieces Quilt
Trip Around the World Quilt
Heart's Delight Wallhanging
Scrap Quilt, Strips and Spider Webs
Rail Fence Quilt
Dresden Placemats
Flying Geese Quilt
Star for all Seasons Placemats
Winning Hand Quilt
Courthouse Steps Quilt
From Blocks to Quilt
Nana's Garden Quilt

Applique

Applique in a Day
Dresden Plate Quilt
Sunbonnet Sue Visits Quilt in a Day
Recycled Treasures
Country Cottages and More
Creating with Color
Spools & Tools Wallhanging
Dutch Windmills Quilt

Intermediate to Advanced

Trio of Treasured Quilts
Lover's Knot Quilt
Amish Quilt
May Basket Quilt
Morning Star Quilt
Friendship Quilt
Kaleidoscope Quilt
Machine Quilting Primer
Tulip Quilt

Star Log Cabin Quilt
Burgoyne Surrounded Quilt
Bird's Eye Quilt
Snowball Quilt
Tulip Table Runner
Triple Irish Chain Quilts
Jewel Box Quilt

Holiday

Country Christmas
Bunnies & Blossoms
Patchwork Santa
Last Minute Gifts
Angel of Antiquity
Log Cabin Wreath Wallhanging
Log Cabin Christmas Tree Wallhanging
Country Flag
Lover's Knot Placemats
Christmas Quilts and Crafts

Sampler

The Sampler
Block Party Series 1, Quilter's Year
Block Party Series 2, Baskets & Flowers
Block Party Series 3, Quilters Almanac
Block Party Series 4, Christmas Traditions
Block Party Series 5, Pioneer Sampler
Block Party Series 7, Stars Across America

Angle Piecing

Diamond Log Cabin Tablecloth or Treeskirt
Pineapple Quilt
Blazing Star Tablecloth
Schoolhouse Quilt
Radiant Star Quilt

Quilt in a Day®, Inc. • 1955 Diamond Street, • San Marcos, CA 92069
Toll Free: 1 800 777-4852 • Fax: (760) 591-4424
Internet: www.quilt-in-a-day.com • 8 am to 5 pm Pacific Time